RAISING TELEPATHIC CHILDREN

A New Guide for Intuition, Energy, and Conscious Parenting

RAISING TELEPATHIC CHILDREN

A New Guide for Intuition, Energy, and Conscious Parenting

Susan V. Whittaker, PhD, DMs, MS

Wellsong Energetics, LLC
1525 Norway ST NE
Salem, OR 97301

WELLSONG
ENERGETICS, LLC

First Edition
January 2026

Paperback ISBN: 978-1-962022-06-4

Printed in the USA by
Amazon Global Publishing

Published by
Wellsong Publishing House
An imprint of Wellsong Energetics, LLC
1525 Norway ST NE
Salem, OR 97301

Disclaimer

The author of this book does not dispense medical or psychological advice, nor prescribe the use of any technique as a form of treatment for any physical, emotional, mental, spiritual, or medical condition. The information provided is intended solely for educational and inspirational purposes. Readers are encouraged to seek the guidance of a qualified physician or licensed therapist or other appropriate professional regarding any health or mental-related concerns. The author and publisher assume no responsibility for the use or misuse of the information contained herein.

ENDORSEMENTS

The programming a child receives before age seven is the primary determinant of that child's health and fate as an adult. Raising Telepathic Children by Susan Whittaker, PhD, provides the current science on how patterns of thoughts and emotions, fundamentally programmed in our earliest life experiences, shape the character of a person's adult life. I encourage all parents and extended family members to read Susan's vital message and insights on how to elicit a child's highest intelligence, integrity, and potential to enhance their lives, as well as that of the planet.

Bruce H. Lipton, Ph.D.
pioneer in epigenetic science
author of the bestselling books: *The Biology of Belief,*
Spontaneous Evolution, and *The Honeymoon Effect*

"Raising Telepathic Children honors the prophesy of the awakened New Human, which I have been teaching for decades. It is the intuitive child born aware, compassionate, and connected to the field."

Lee Carroll
Author of *The Indigo Children*, Hay House 1999

"Every parent needs this book, and I am so glad you wrote it."

Dr. Bradley Nelson
author of the bestselling books:
The Emotion Code®, *The Body Code, The, Belief Code*®, *and The Heart Code*®

We really like this book—timely and important. It's a must-have for parents who want to start working with our so-important, almost forgotten ability to communicate on nonverbal levels. *Raising Telepathic Children* beautifully shows how vibration, coherence, and subtle energy shape a child's intuitive awareness. Susan offers a compassionate and practical guide for families ready to embrace a more conscious and connected way of living.

Andi and Jonathan Goldman
Pioneers in sound healing and vibroacoustic resonance
Authors of *The Humming Effect*

In *Raising Telepathic Children*, Susan brings forward a rare and important synthesis of science and experience. Using the principles of the living matrix, coherence, and energetic communication, she demonstrates that children are exquisitely sensitive to the fields around them. This book offers an inspired and practical framework for supporting these natural abilities. Her work aligns beautifully with the growing biophysical understanding of the human biofield.

James L. Oschman, PhD
world authority on Energy Medicine
author of *Energy Medicine: The Scientific Basis,* and
Energy Medicine in Therapeutics and Human Performance

DEDICATION

To the pioneers and path-clearers:

Veda Austin

Gregg Braden

Lee Carroll

Margaret Horton

Dr. Bruce Lipton

Dr. Bradley Nelson

Dr. Beverly Rubik

Thank you for helping me trust the unseen and remember the power within. Thank you for showing the world that energy and water remember us, just as we are learning to remember them.

And thank you to every child who never forgot, and to every parent, teacher, caregiver, and healer listening to my message—together, we are advancing the quality of life on earth.

This is for you.

ACKNOWLEDGEMENTS

This book combines many voices that have guided, inspired, and confirmed the path of remembering. To these visionaries who bridge energy and evidence, faith and physiology, intuition and intellect, I offer my deepest gratitude. They illuminate the way for parents, teachers, and caregivers to see that what connects us has never been lost. It's waiting to be remembered.

This book could not exist without the paths they cleared and truths they have discovered and shared with love and hope. It is with deepest gratitude and reverence that I honor their lifetime contributions to this unfolding evolution of the human heart.

To Dr. Bruce H. Lipton:

Your work opened the doorway between science and spirit. Through your pioneering research on consciousness, biology, and belief, you gave us language for what the heart has always known—that our thoughts shape our cells and that love is the highest frequency of healing. This book builds on the connections you discovered.

To Lee Carroll, the voice of KRYON:

Thank you for carrying the light of remembrance so faithfully. Your channelings have inspired millions to trust their inner wisdom and see the divine pattern within humanity. Your echo of "children still see the other side" felt like a joyful confirmation from the field itself, affirming that the message of this book was already being heard across dimensions.

To Dr. Bradley Nelson:

Your devotion to transforming countless lives through the Emotion Code®, Body Code®, Belief Code®, and Heart Code® defines a clear and compassionate map for freeing the heart. This book honors your legacy of love in motion.

FOREWORD

As someone who has devoted my life to helping people release trapped emotions and reconnect with their true selves, I recognize that the most profound healing happens not through complex techniques, but through restoring our natural ability to feel, sense, and communicate from the heart.

Dr. Susan Whittaker has given families an extraordinary gift with Raising Telepathic Children. This book gently reminds us of what children have always known—that we can connect with each other beyond words, through energy, emotion, and presence. Before we learned to speak, we communicated through vibration. Before we were taught to doubt our intuition, we simply knew.

Sue's work beautifully bridges ancient wisdom with modern understanding. Having spent decades teaching children and witnessing their innate intuitive abilities, she writes with both compassion and clarity. The practical tools throughout this book—from the Telepathy Toolbox games to the energy programming practices—make this profound subject accessible to every parent, educator, and caregivers who longs to support the children in their care.

What moved me most about this book is how it honors the simplicity of love. You don't need to be psychic or specially trained to connect telepathically with your child. You simply need to trust what you feel, create space for what cannot be spoken, and remember that your heart has always known how to listen.

The children who walk among us today carry tremendous light. They are sensitive, aware, and deeply attuned to the energy around them. When we help them keep their channels open—and when we reopen our own—we participate in something sacred: the remembering of who we truly are.

This book is not just about raising telepathic children. It's about healing the communication between generations, restoring trust in our inner knowing, and building families where love can be felt even in the silence.

Every parent needs this book. Whether your child is verbal or nonverbal, sensitive or outgoing, struggling or thriving, the practices within these pages will transform how you connect. In a world that so often misunderstands our children's gifts, Susan shows us how to see them clearly, honor their wisdom, and meet them in the language their souls already speak.

I wholeheartedly recommend *Raising Telepathic Children* to anyone who believes, as I do, that true healing begins with the heart.

Dr. Bradley Nelson
Creator of The Emotion Code®, The Body Code®,
The Heart Code®, and The Belief Code®
Founder, Discover Healing, Inc.

NOTE TO READERS

Dear Reader,

If you have made it here, something in your heart has remembered.

This book was not written to teach you something new but to awaken something ancient: something already living in your bones, your breath, your being—and to help you keep it active and growing.

I awoke one morning and this entire book was laid out in my mind. I understood the metaphysical training I received from shamans, from infancy to adulthood, was the key to my success teaching Indian and Eskimo children. They had been taught to communicate telepathically.

I also knew the natural capacity for communicating and knowing can be recovered and fluently used by others.

I was told to hurry and waste no time. The world is ready for *The Remembering*.

Telepathy is a dimension of the Creator of All. The words that gave birth to the universe were spoken with telepathic intention. It nurtures and refines the love between parents, children and helpers in creative and eternal ways. Telepathy promotes individualization and maturation. It guides us toward the fullness of our soul.

Whether you are a parent, partner, teacher, healer, caregiver or a soul simply walking through the world, you were called to this book.

You may have cried at a child's dream. You may have felt a stirring while reading a story. You may have whispered, "I've always known this." That whisper is the thread that ties you to the field of remembering and to the telepathic ones who walk quietly beside us.

Please do not let this be the end. Let it be a beginning. Speak to your children in silence. Gaze into their eyes longer than is practical and invite silent communication. Be present. Let them lead you at times, not with words, but with clues that invite a deeper conversation.

If you are the child reading this with grown-up hands, know that I see you in a way you can feel, but cannot explain.

You never forgot.

Thank you for helping the rest of us remember.

With love,
Sue

HOW TO USE THIS BOOK
A GUIDE TO REMEMBERING WHAT YOU ALREADY KNOW

This is a workbook that helps parents help their children keep their telepathy alive and helps parents remember their own. It is laid out in three parts designed to deepen understanding through reflection, science, and practice:

- Part 1: The Child
- Part 2: The Parent
- Part 3: The Remembering

Each part includes several recurring features described with more detail in Appendix D - Quick Start Guide. I recommend you read that and get the deeper guidance it holds before starting this journey.

- **Science Notes** – provide background for those who want to explore further. Because telepathy is often dismissed in mainstream research, these sections help you navigate what's possible and what's not.

- **Practitioner Prompts** – offer questions and perspectives for teachers, caregivers, healers, and anyone working with children beyond their own.

- **Invitations** – encourage awareness, reflection and self-assessment as your world of knowing expands.

- **Telepathic Toolbox** – presents simple, verifiable communication exercises and settings for practice. The exercises can be skipped or done in any order, at any time. They may unfold gradually; sessions that feel unsuccessful may yield insight as you remember.

- **Transmissions from the Telepathic Ones** – are direct messages of guidance and love received for this book, inviting you into a deeper connection with the unseen world. They are written with the sense of what was said and how it was expressed.

INTRODUCTION
YOUR FORGOTTEN LANGUAGE

It seems like I have lived in three different worlds throughout my life. In my current world, I have worked in 70 Costco stores, as well as countless trade shows, expos, and conferences. I have been to all 50 states, plus Japan, Canada, many Caribbean islands, and several countries in Central America. In doing so, I have flown over a million miles and met about 500,000 people. My sense of telepathy led to me setting sales records and, often, my husband would call to ask if I was thinking of him, because I had just woken him up.

In a conversation one day, my telepathic nature was noted by a professor who taught astronauts in Houston, TX. Quite unexpectedly, he warned me and taught me how to block others from reading my mind!

In the middle part of my life, I worked in the structured world of public education. I taught first grade for 25 years and taught other teachers from preschool through high school how to use computers and enhance their success. Many said I was gifted given the knowledge and skills my students gained. Looking back, I owe much of that to the common use of telepathy in my first world.

I grew up in an Athabascan village of 80 people in the center of Alaska where silent communication traveled faster than speech, and truth vibrated with distinctive frequencies. I learned about the meaning and joy of life in silent, profound exchanges. I didn't learn telepathy there. I just didn't lose it. I will tell you more about village life in a moment.

Though these three worlds seem separate, I have come to understand they are deeply intertwined. In fact, I believe they are part of this book's core message: children are born telepathic, but we teach them to forget.

As a bridge between these worlds, I have earned a Ph.D. and a Doctorate of Metaphysical Science, along with a Master's in Early Childhood Education with a focus on first grade. That's where the deepest magic occurs. It's the borderland where children begin to lose their natural telepathic abilities and adopt verbal language as their primary communication style. Halfway through first grade, something would change. While striving for each student's success, I did not understand the shift or the silent effects until recently. You may sense the shift too.

Sometimes, You Do Not Just See It. You Feel It.

When my daughter was two years old, we had taped pictures of colors and words to the shelves in our living room. She could identify every color, match them to words, and soon after, read. By age three, she was decoding books. We did not teach her to read. She listened. She observed. And more than that, she picked up what we were thinking. She understood not just what we said, but what we were thinking.

My son has a similar gift. The first time he held a fiddle he could play it. Not by chance, not by trial and error. He had watched others play, and apparently, he "read their minds" to know where to put his fingers. He was not copying. He was tuning in or was reincarnated, or both. He was 5 years old.

In my classroom, I saw this same phenomenon again and again. One boy, who had been labeled ADHD in kindergarten, could tell me each morning which dinosaur we were going to study before I introduced the lesson. I taught one new dinosaur each day, and somehow, he always knew which one it would be. It was as if he were pulling the thought straight from my mind. I worked closely with his parents to remove him from all medications, because I knew this child did not need to be suppressed. He needed to be supported. He was not a problem. He was a prophet in miniature.

Another child, quiet and artistic, would ask his classmates to think of an animal. Then, he'd draw it. Every time, he got it right. We did not call it autism back then, but today he might fall into that category. What I saw was not a diagnosis, it was brilliance. He had access to something most of us, by his age, had already lost.

I understand that loss. I was born with telepathy too and still have it. I regularly finish people's sentences. I set sales records in Costco stores across the country. I could spot buyers as they walked in the door a hundred feet away and tell a co-worker, "That man with the blue shirt is going to buy one of these." To her utter amazement, I was always right. Clairvoyance, telepathy, precognition? I do not know which. It was just a knowing, and I often sense people's preferences, reasoning, questions, and emotions as clearly as if spoken aloud. I've always trusted and followed my inner voice, that energetic "knowing."

As you practice the lessons in this book you will start to understand that telepathy is not rare. It is mostly unrecognized and misunderstood. It can be very useful but also challenging to discern. When telepathy has gone unnoticed for decades, inner knowing and simple thoughts become blurred. The toolbox activities and games in this book can enhance your awareness of those around you and sustain the gifts of love in your life.

Frequencies of Health and Longevity

My interest in metaphysics, frequency, and healing led me to developing a line of non-consumable homeopathic remedies that lower the risks of chronic disease. This breakthrough discovery came through the recognition that the laws of physics control how chemistry works. Health and longevity require balanced energy and natural frequencies. As with telepathy, what we cannot see is often more significant than what we can. There is more about this in Appendix E. The Broad Spectrum DeTOX Program

Village Life, Shamans and Telepathy

My village had no sidewalks, no roads, no stores, no hotels, no restaurants. There was an air-taxi service operated by Don Sheldon, a pioneering icon of early aviation.

I was surrounded by silence, wooded wilderness, energy and ancestral wisdom. There were no TVs. No movies. No distractions. The few crank-operated phones were on a party line, so everyone could eavesdrop and keep up on "village news."

My father was the air traffic controller for the brave bush pilots. He also watched the sky with defensive radar to alert others whenever Russian bombers challenged our readiness by flying too close.

My father used ham radio equipment to make friends in distant parts of the world. No place was too far away. At the age of three, before I could read, I was making friends through the sound of "dots and dashes" known as Morse code—the precursor to texting.

Once a week, a train would stop at our tiny village sitting at the foot of Mt. McKinley, the highest and the most challenging climbing excursion in North America. The train would bring "funny people" from distant places to climb the mountain, and later, take them away. The visitors brought skis and walking sticks along with huge backpacks stuffed with tools and food. They were dressed in unusual clothing. When they spoke, I heard strange sounds, yet it seemed like I understood them.

My curiosity about the rest of the world grew to enormous proportions, which may explain why I travel so much, talk with so many people, and am very perceptive and telepathic.

The visitors brought little change to village life; the ancient culture was stored and preserved in this small group of authentic people. The elders had taught them well for millennia and they were surviving against harsh odds. I, too, was taught by the elders and shamans. I used to visit the three shamans and "play" at their humble homes. They showed me how to find herbs, how to listen to the land, and how to make and use healing remedies for others in the village. I learned from them how to trust the earth and my own instincts.

They shared their wisdom and taught me their trades so I could pass it on. I was immersed in a culture of love and compassion I cannot describe. Reverence for nature and its lessons filled each moment and guided every act and every thought, in everyone in the village every day. At forty below, the will to survive is stark, bold and strong. In the summer, life, love and joyfulness permeated gathering and preparing for the coming winter.

As I grew older, my family and I traveled through Canada on the Alaskan Highway to the "lower 48" and searched through petrified forests for their hidden treasures and other areas rich with dinosaur bones.

I became a teacher and spent a decade living in Yup'ik Eskimo villages along the Bering Sea. They had less contact with "outsiders" than the villagers of my youth. There were no visitors other than an occasional nurse or dentist. The word Yup'ik means "People." I witnessed the fading past of a nomadic people. The people were playful and had a sense of oneness that drove every thought and action. In their world, a forgotten ancestral lesson could cause lives to be lost. Their sense of an inseparable oneness demanded cooperation, foresight and charity. Alaskan natives have a firm rule: when you pass through a temporary location, leave it in better condition than how it was when you first arrived. (e. g. replace the fire wood that was there to keep you warm—or go back soon and do so.) This made survival possible, and it is sadly missing in the world today.

Survival was not just about food or fire. It was about connection. And intuition was not a luxury. It was a necessity. I believe that lack of a common language helped me hone my telepathic abilities and, later, recognize them in the children I would teach.

I remember how easy it was to read my mother's thoughts but not my father's. I never figured that out. He died when I was 13. He was raised in an Indian tribe and probably knew more about telepathy than I do today. As I grew older, I wondered why. Was it frequency? Was it emotion? Was it trust? All of those questions led me deeper into my spiritual path and eventually to the doctoral work that merged my intuition and wisdom lessons from the elders with the science and technology I learned from my dad, and others along this journey.

The Power of the Mind

And then there's the brain science: the part that makes all of this not just mystical, but measurable.

Dr. Bruce Lipton, a developmental biologist and author of The Biology of Belief: Unleashing the Power of Consciousness, Matter, and Miracles often quotes the Jesuits: "Give me the child until he is seven and I will give you the man." Lipton explains that children's minds operate in theta brainwave states until about age seven. Their brains are highly receptive, imaginative, and deeply programmable. Theta is the same brainwave associated with hypnosis and intuition. It is the state where beliefs are formed and the subconscious is most open and receptive.

In his words, a child's mind before age 7 is like wet concrete and accepts impressions from everything and everyone. But I want to add this: that same state of receptivity allows them to access information non-locally and beyond the five senses. It allows them to feel, hear, and see thoughts as if they were spoken aloud. This ability started in-utero and was not simply prelinguistic but it was "chemical words" that surrounded them from the mother's biology of belief, her perceptions and her interpretation of her world. She "spoke" chemically to the developing embryo.

This is telepathy. It's not the Hollywood version, but the gentle, invisible, deeply human way. It does not just exist; it thrives in childhood until being discouraged and suppressed.

This book does not just link education and intuition; it links the families, cultures and societies.

It's for parents, educators, grandparents, caregivers, healers, researchers and even skeptics. It is for anyone who has looked into a child's eyes and felt the unmistakable knowing that passes without words.

This book is not designed to teach children or their parents how to be telepathic. It's to help them remember that they are already telepathic. And in helping others remember, we too will remember.

Welcome back to the subtle, perfect language before words.

My brain is only a receiver. In the universe, there is a core from which we obtain knowledge, strength, and inspiration.

— Nikola Tesla

CONTENTS

Bonus Section

Author Section

PART ONE:
THE CHILD

Children do not learn telepathy.
They remember it.

— *Anonymous*

CHAPTER 1

Born Knowing: The Telepathic Infant

Before an infant utters a single word, before they grasp language or form a conscious memory, they are already communicating. And not just through crying, cooing, or clinging. They are engaging in a far more subtle, sophisticated, and ancient form of communication: telepathy. It is the forgotten language of the soul, and every child is born fluent.

Telepathy, simply defined, is the direct exchange of thoughts, feelings, or images between two beings without the use of spoken words. It is often dismissed as a paranormal phenomenon, yet in the realm of early childhood development, and especially in the spiritual domain, telepathy is not only real; it is essential. While empathy is the ability to feel another's emotions, telepathy is the ability to receive them as thoughts, sensations, or imagery before they are expressed.

In fact, the earliest stages of life are immersed in it. Before birth, during birth, and well into the first years of life, children reside in a brainwave state that supports heightened intuition and energetic awareness. It is not imagination; it is not guessing. It is perception in its purest form.

The Theta Brainwave Connection

From conception through about age seven, a child's dominant brainwave state is theta. This frequency range, between 4-8 Hz, is the same state accessed during hypnosis, deep meditation, and intuitive downloads. In adults, theta is a bridge between the conscious and subconscious minds. In children, it is home.

In this theta state, children are highly impressionable, deeply imaginative, and energetically open. They absorb information not just

3

through the senses, but through vibrational fields. This is why young children can learn languages rapidly, mimic behaviors effortlessly, and "know" things they were never explicitly taught.

But beyond their learning capacity, theta brainwaves allow children to operate in what could be called a natural telepathic state. Their boundaries are fluid. Their identity is still merging with the environment. In this space, thoughts are shared as feelings, and feelings as energy.

As Bruce Lipton explains in *The Biology of Belief: Unleashing the Power of Consciousness, Matter, and Miracles*, the subconscious mind, which is most active in the theta state, is programmed before the age of seven. Children are essentially living in a continuous download state, absorbing not only spoken messages but energetic patterns. This explains why telepathic perception is so natural and potent during early life.

Developmental author Joseph Chilton Pearce called this period the *magical mind*, describing early childhood as a dreamlike state of openness where children learn by resonance and feeling more than by logic.

In Utero: The First Bonds

Long before a child takes their first breath, they are already tuned to the energetic environment around them. Science confirms that by the second trimester, a fetus can hear and respond to sound. But sound is only one layer. Babies in utero recognize vibration, tone, and most importantly, frequency.

Every person has a unique vibrational signature. This includes mothers, fathers, siblings, and even grandparents. Babies attune to these frequencies while still in the womb. They sense joy, stress, fear, and love from their mothers, not just chemically through cortisol or oxytocin, but energetically, through the field.

Neuroscientist Allan Schore has shown that this kind of nonverbal emotional attunement between mother and infant is actually what regulates the baby's developing nervous system. In other words, the baby is not only listening for words or touch—it is tuning to the mother's emotional frequency.

4

And It Goes Further

Mothers often report feeling a baby's response to external emotions or thoughts. If the father walks into the room and thinks about the baby, the fetus kicks. If a sibling talks to the belly, the baby shifts or settles. These are not random movements: they are telepathic exchanges.

Some mothers have vivid dreams where their unborn child communicates with them, sometimes telling them their name, gender, or a message of reassurance. Others report knowing something was wrong or right, long before medical scans could confirm it. These are not isolated incidents. They are part of a hidden truth: in utero, children are not just biological beings; they are energetic beings already in communication with the people they are destined to love.

Siblings and Soul Connection

Telepathic bonds between siblings are particularly strong. Even before they meet in the physical world, their souls are often in communication.

Older siblings may begin to talk to the unborn baby with an intensity that surprises parents. Sometimes, they "know" the baby's name or refer to them with astonishing accuracy. One child might tell their mother, "My sister said she's ready to come out now," just hours before labor begins. Another might wake up crying the same night their sibling has a medical issue in the womb.

These stories are common among intuitive families. The siblings are not making it up. They are connected. Soul families often incarnate together, and telepathic awareness between them is part of the soul contract.

Mother-Infant Resonance

After birth, the most well-documented and universally accepted form of nonverbal connection is the bond between mother and child. While modern science may focus on skin-to-skin contact and oxytocin release, the metaphysical reality is that the mother-infant connection is a telepathic relationship.

5

Mothers often "know" when their child is about to wake up, even from another room. They sense when something is wrong, even before a cry is heard. They feel distress, excitement, or hunger at a distance. Some mothers report "phantom letdowns." These are sensations in the breast as milk releases when the baby is upset, even if they are not nursing.

These are not coincidences. They are a type of energetic umbilical cord that persists beyond the physical one. This cord allows for the constant exchange of emotional information, needs, images, and impulses. Over time, this telepathic line is often buried beneath routines, schedules, and spoken commands; but in the earliest days, it is the dominant mode of connection.

Harvard psychiatrist John Ratey, MD, emphasizes that the infant brain is extraordinarily plastic, meaning it wires itself according to the emotional environment. When a mother consistently sends signals of safety and love, those patterns become embedded in the child's neural architecture.

The Silent Language of Emotion

Infants communicate through more than cries and cues. A baby may begin crying the moment a parent has an upsetting thought. They may suddenly calm when a parent silently projects feelings of safety. Some parents report their newborns watching them intently during moments of internal conflict, as if reading the internal conversation.

In fact, babies are extremely sensitive to internal states. You can be smiling, singing, and swaddling, but if your mind is racing with fear or doubt, the baby will react. They are not responding to your behavior. They are responding to your frequency.

This is telepathy in its truest form: not reading surface thoughts like words on a page, but receiving the entire emotional field being emitted by another. In infancy, children are still deeply connected to Source and spirit. They have not yet formed the illusion of separation, and so they receive emotion as information.

How Telepathic Communication Works

Telepathy is not about "mind-reading" in the traditional sense. It is about vibrational resonance. Every thought has a frequency. Every feeling sends out a wave. When two beings are attuned, especially through love, blood, or soul contract, those waves transmit clearly.

For infants, who have not yet learned to block, filter, or doubt, the reception is wide open. Their auric field is expansive, their chakras are spinning freely, and their pineal gland is still uncalcified and active. They receive through multiple channels:

How Infants Receive Telepathic Messages

Here is a list of the primary telepathic channels:

- Emotion – felt as waves or internal resonance
- Imagery – dreamlike mental pictures or inner visuals
- Aura Interaction – information exchanged through the energy field
- Tone & Intention – the meaning behind words is more impactful than the words themselves
- Environmental Energy – tension, joy, or peace in a room can be felt and mirrored by the infant

Stories from the Field

Parents often share remarkable stories that defy explanation:

- A baby who cried inconsolably every time a certain person entered the room, until that person resolved a hidden anger they had never shared.
- A newborn who would only calm down when their father, while still at work, mentally visualized holding them and sending love.
- A mother who "heard" her baby ask her to move to a quieter place before birth, and who later realized that environmental stress had been affecting them both.

What I Noticed with My Own Children

When my daughter was little, I would imagine a lightbulb over my head as if an idea was forming; then I'd silently project an image to her to see if she would respond. She often did. If I pictured her teddy bear, she would bring it to me. If I visualized a certain snack, she would ask for it. It became a little game between us; two lightbulbs passing ideas across invisible space. What amazed me most was how natural it was for her; as if she was not learning it at all, but remembering it.

My son, too, displayed early signs of this silent language. He learned to fiddle not by being taught, but by watching, and it was not just imitation. He somehow felt where the notes were supposed to go, and it showed in his ability to play songs intuitively. In many ways, I believe my children taught me more about telepathy than any book ever could.

Why We Forget

As children grow and develop, language becomes dominant. Logic is prioritized. The intuitive, right-brain mode of connection is slowly replaced with vocabulary tests and behavior charts. Cultural conditioning tells children what is "real" and what is "just your imagination." Pearce warned that when adults dismiss imagination, they are often dismissing the child's deepest mode of perception—symbolic and intuitive knowing.

By age seven, the dominant brainwave state shifts from theta to alpha and beta states of alertness and critical thinking. While this is a natural progression, it also marks the beginning of what many call "the forgetting."

But not all is lost.

Some children retain strong telepathic abilities well into adolescence. Others experience spontaneous reactivations later in life. And parents, when supported and attuned, can preserve this sacred channel of communication much longer than we think.

Science Note

From conception through about age seven, children's brains operate predominantly in the theta-wave state (4–8 Hz). This is the same frequency range accessed in deep meditation, hypnosis, and states of heightened intuition. In this dreamlike condition, children absorb not just words, but entire patterns of behavior, emotion, and energy.

Cell biologist Bruce Lipton, Ph.D. has shown that during these years, the subconscious mind is wide open, "downloading" beliefs and impressions from the environment. Developmental researcher Joseph Chilton Pearce described this same period as a "magical state of consciousness," where the child's mind is open, fluid, and shaped more by feelings than logic. Neuroscientist Allan Schore, Ph.D. has demonstrated that infants regulate their developing nervous systems through nonverbal emotional attunement with caregivers, confirming that feeling is their first language. Psychiatrist John Ratey, M.D. emphasizes the brain's extraordinary plasticity in this period, explaining that children's perceptions and emotional environments directly sculpt the neural pathways they will carry for life.

In this receptive theta field, children do not merely learn; they know. They resonate, absorb, and remember in ways that reveal the natural telepathic state of early life.

Practitioner Prompt

If you are working with a new parent or caregiver, try this: Invite them to spend five minutes a day silently sending love, calm, or imagery to their infant; no speaking, just feeling. Ask them to journal the baby's responses for one week. What patterns emerge? What shifts?

Telepathy Toolbox

Why Toolbox Activities Matter for Children and Adults

When parents and caregivers practice vibrational awareness, it shapes the way children grow and connect. Children raised in this environment feel more seen and understood, remain connected to their inner knowing, and naturally develop empathy, intuition, and creativity.

Most importantly, they do not forget the *Language of Light*—because no one tells them to abandon it. You are not just teaching your child to talk; you are helping them remember who they truly are.

The first activities are ways parents, siblings, and family members can notice and support the telepathic connection that is already alive in infants. They are not about creating something new, but about recognizing what is already present. Try them as playful bonding activities, and observe what changes when you begin to listen with more than words.

Let this activity become a regularly scheduled routine, if possible, to convey the importance of the connection and the time spent together. The routine will set up positive feelings and anticipation which in will improve connectedness before you even sit down together.

Quick Setup & Timing Tips:
- Environment: low light, soft voice, few distractions.
- Duration: infants tire fast; 1–3 minutes per game is perfect.
- Frequency: 1–2 practices a day is better than long sessions.
- Stop cues: yawns, looking away, stiffening, it's time to pause/try later.

Heart-Listening Telepathy

Help your child understand telepathy as a natural form of caring awareness they already use—without making it mystical, scary, or confusing.

How to do it:

1. Sit together quietly for a moment—no pressure, just openness.
2. Say: "Telepathy is when you can feel what someone else feels, even without words."
3. Share simple, everyday examples:
4. "Remember when you knew I needed a hug?"
5. "Have you felt a friend was sad even when they smiled?"
6. Invite your child to guess what you're feeling right now (happy, calm, excited, tired).
7. Switch roles and let them share how they feel inside.
8. Gently add: "We never use telepathy to get into someone's private thoughts. It's about kindness and caring."

Why it works:

Children already use intuitive awareness—they just need a name for it.

By connecting telepathy to familiar experiences and emotions, you show them it's a natural extension of empathy, not a supernatural power. This activity also creates opportunities to teach values such as respect, privacy, and kindness while strengthening your emotional bond.

The Quiet Heart Game

Help your child slow down, tune in, and discover that telepathy often begins as a soft, shared feeling in the heart rather than a clear thought in the mind.

How to do it:

1. Sit together quietly in a peaceful spot—no goals, no expectations.

2. Invite your child to place a hand over their own heart while you place a hand over yours.

3. Say softly: "Let's see if we can feel what our hearts are saying right now."

4. Close your eyes for 10–15 seconds and breathe slowly.

5. Ask your child: "What does your heart feel like? Calm? Warm? Bouncy? Quiet?"

6. Then ask: "What do you think my heart feels like?"

7. Switch roles so they tell you what you might be feeling.

8. Share gently: "Telepathy isn't about reading thoughts. It's about noticing feelings and caring about each other."

Why it works:

Children experience emotions as energy before they ever form words.

This activity teaches them that telepathy begins with connection, presence, and shared awareness, not pressure or performance. It also strengthens empathy and creates a peaceful bonding ritual you can return to again and again.

Feel-What-I-Feel Game

A simple, playful way for children to tune into someone else's emotional state while learning healthy boundaries and kindness.

How to do it:

1. Sit facing each other or side-by-side.

2. Say: "I'm going to feel one feeling inside—let's see if you can sense which one it is."

3. Choose a simple emotion (happy, tired, peaceful, excited) and focus on it for 5–7 seconds.

4. Invite your child to guess by naming a feeling, drawing a quick symbol, or pointing to a facial expression.

5. Affirm any part they sensed correctly ("Yes! I was calm," or "You picked up on the tired part!").

6. Switch roles and let your child choose a feeling for you to sense.

7. End by saying: "Telepathy works best when we listen with our hearts, not just our minds."

Why it works:

Children are often already attuned to emotional states—they just need permission to trust what they notice.

This game teaches emotional intelligence, safe attunement, and relational awareness, helping them recognize that telepathy is most powerful when it comes from care, not accuracy.

Telepathy & Body Language Matching Game

Help your child understand the difference between what we see and what we feel—an essential skill for telepathy, empathy, and navigating complex social cues.

How to do it:

1. Sit together where you can see each other clearly.
2. Say: "Sometimes people show one feeling on the outside but feel something different on the inside. Let's practice noticing both."
3. Choose a simple outward expression (smile, frown, neutral look).
4. nervous, happy, tired).
5. Hold that expression while quietly feeling a different inner emotion (calm, nervous, happy, tired).\
6. Ask your child two questions:
   o "What does my face look like I'm feeling?"
   o "What does your heart feel like I'm really feeling?"
7. Switch roles so your child gets to "show" one feeling and "feel" another.
8. End with: "Telepathy helps us understand feelings beneath the surface. And we always use it with kindness."

Why it works:

This game teaches children that body language is physical, while telepathy is relational.

It helps them become sensitive to emotional mismatch, which reduces confusion, increases empathy, and teaches them to trust subtle impressions over appearances.

Sibling Connection Game

A bonding activity that helps siblings feel united, important to one another, and connected through shared intuition—especially helpful when jealousy or competition is present.

How to do it:

1. Invite both siblings to sit together in a quiet, safe space.
2. Say: "Let's see how well your hearts talk to each other without words."
3. Ask one sibling to silently think of a simple image (sun, teddy bear, tree, heart).
4. Both place a hand over their hearts and breathe slowly together for 5 seconds.
5. Invite the other sibling to guess the image, draw it, or choose from a few picture cards.
6. Celebrate any part that feels close, even symbolically—"You picked a circle, and they imagined the sun! That's amazing teamwork."
7. Switch roles so each sibling gets a turn to send and receive.
8. End by saying: "You two have a strong connection. When you listen with your hearts, you can feel each other clearly."

Why it works:

This game transforms sibling dynamics from competition to collaboration. It lets older children feel important, helps younger children feel seen, and builds a quiet bond where telepathy becomes a shared superpower rather than something that divides attention.

Lightbulb Images

Invite your infant or toddler to "catch" a simple picture you are holding in mind.

How to do it:

1. Sit near your baby in a calm, quiet space.
2. Choose a very familiar object (teddy, bottle, blanket, banana).
3. Close your eyes for 3 breaths, then picture it vividly (size, color, feel).

   - Softly look at your child and mentally "shine" the image like a little lightbulb above your head.
   - Wait 10–20 seconds. If your child reaches, looks toward, or crawls to the object, notice it; if not, gently show the object and smile.
   - Switch images or end after ~2 minutes. Jot any patterns you notice.

Why it works:

Babies track images, feeling-tones, and intention long before words. Repetition with beloved objects helps them associate your inner picture with a felt cue of "that one!"

Silent Soothing

Co-regulate your baby by sending calm without words.

How to do it:

1. Place a hand lightly over your heart; rest the other hand near (or on) baby's belly/blanket (only if it is welcome).
2. Breathe: inhale 4, exhale 6, for 6–10 cycles.
3. Imagine a color of calm (soft blue, warm gold) filling your chest, then flowing gently toward your baby.
4. Silently think one phrase (e.g., "Safe and loved") for 20–30 seconds.

5. Notice subtle cues: softer eyes, slower breath, relaxed hands. If baby fusses, pause and try again later.

6. Log times of day when this works best.

Why it works:

Your rhythm and emotional state are cues your baby reads instantly. Calm, coherent breathing + a steady inner picture gives the body a clear signal of safety.

Sibling Soul Talk

Let older siblings discover they can "send a message" to baby—then draw the reply.

How to do it:

1. Invite the sibling to sit quietly beside baby for 30–60 seconds.

2. Ask them to think one simple feeling or picture (e.g., "I love you," a smiley sun, "nap time").

3. Have them send the feeling/picture silently to baby for ~10–15 seconds.

4. Right away, both of you draw what baby 'said back'—a color, a symbol, or a scribble.

5. Share your drawings and celebrate any overlaps or fun surprises.

Why it works:

Symbols and feelings are a child's first language. Siblings gain confidence seeing that silent connection can be noticed and shared—on paper!

Dream Sharing

Honor family dreams (including pre-birth impressions) as valid messages.

How to do it:

1. Keep a small notebook by the bed.

2. In the morning, **draw or jot** any image, color, or feeling you remember, even one word. Date each entry.

3. Ask partners/siblings if they had any feelings or dreams about baby (before or after birth).

4. Once a week, flip back together and circle repeating symbols/colors.

Why it works:

Dreams often mirror shared emotions and anticipations. Recording them shows the whole family that inner experiences matter—and patterns emerge.

Pre-Verbal Check-In

Pause to "listen" to baby's state before acting.

How to do it:

1. Stop for one breath. Place a hand on your heart or the edge of the crib.

2. Silently ask: *"What do you need—comfort, food, change, quiet, or rest?"*

3. Notice an **instant impression** (an image, a word, an urge).

4. Try the most likely action first (e.g., adjust light, pick up, offer bottle).

5. Reflect for 10 seconds: did the energy settle? If yes, you got it.

Why it works:

That first felt sense is often accurate. This trains your nervous system to catch subtle signals before they escalate into cries.

Emotion Echo Cards

Use simple cards to practice sending and sensing feelings without words.

How to do it:

1. Make 6–10 cards (faces, swirls, shapes), then assign each a feeling (e.g., blue wave = calm; red spiral = mad).

2. Parent picks a card **secretly** and **feels** that state for ~10 seconds.

3. Hold up the set and let baby/toddler **reach** or child **choose** the one they "felt."

4. Name the feeling gently ("You picked calm!"), then **switch roles** with an older child.

5. Keep it light—notice any patterns over time.

Why it works:

Pairing a symbol with a felt state helps children label and trust inner experience. You are building emotional literacy through color and shape, not lectures.

Toolbox Wrap-Up

These are not tests; they are tiny doorways into a language your baby already speaks. Celebrate any small response, keep notes lightly, and end while it is still fun. The more you practice *presence over performance*, the clearer your family's silent conversation becomes.

What if we began to trust this silent language again? What if we taught new parents that telepathy is not a fantasy, but both a biological and spiritual reality? What if we created space for children to keep their intuitive channels open?

The first step is remembrance. You do not have to *teach* your infant to communicate telepathically. They already know how. Your role is simply to listen differently: to feel beneath the surface, to speak not only with your words but with your presence, and to recognize that every emotion you carry, every thought you hold, is already a message your child receives.

They were born knowing. And deep down, you still remember, too.

Invitation

Let this be your reminder: you are already fluent in the unspoken language of love. Telepathy with your infant is not something to force, teach, or analyze. It is something to remember. Each day, choose presence over pressure. Let your thoughts soften into feelings, and your feelings become the bridge. The more you trust the silent connection, the stronger it becomes. You are not just parenting a body; you are bonding with a soul.

Transmission from the Telepathic Ones

You remember us in lullabies and skin-to-skin warmth.

You heard us before you heard your name.

The softest part of you still listens.

Let it lead.

Speak without words and we will meet you in the space between.

Up Next

To understand this ancient form of communication, we must explore how thoughts form before language ever arrives. That stretches our understanding of how the mind works.

CHAPTER 2

Thought Before Language

Before children learn to speak, they are already fluent in a language far older and more encompassing than words. This language is made of images, sensations, emotions, and energetic impressions. It is the original interface through which they experience the world. It is how they understand and are understood. And for the first few years of life, it is their primary mode of communication.

Modern neuroscience and metaphysics intersect here; both agree that the earliest years of life are governed not by logic or speech, but by perception, emotion, and energetic resonance. Bruce Lipton, PhD, refers to this as a time when the subconscious mind is a sponge, open, impressionable, and responsive to frequency rather than logic. Joseph Chilton Pearce emphasized that play and imagination are biological necessities in early childhood, providing a developmental bridge between emotion and intellect. To understand this hidden layer of childhood is to step back into a way of knowing that is more direct, more expansive, and often more accurate than words will ever allow.

Brain Development and Right-Brain Dominance

In early childhood, the brain is developing rapidly. Neurologically, infants and toddlers operate with significant dominance in the right hemisphere of the brain. The right brain is responsible for intuition, sensory processing, emotional memory, and holistic perception. It does not deal in language, logic, or linear time. Instead, it processes the world as a rich field of impressions and relationships.

This is why young children learn best through play, music, rhythm, color, and movement. These *right-brain* activities allow them to engage with life on an intuitive level. When a toddler hears a song or watches

21

someone dance, they do not just observe, they feel it. The experience becomes part of their internal world.

Only later does the left brain begin to take the lead in processing. This hemisphere is responsible for verbal language, categorization, analysis, and sequential thought. As it becomes more active around age six or seven, children begin to rely more on words than impressions. But in the early years, children are living entirely in the language of feeling and frequency.

The Preverbal Mind: What Happens Before Words

Long before a child speaks, they are immersed in a world of meaning. They recognize tone, intent, and emotion long before they understand vocabulary. A baby may not know the word *anger*, but they feel the sharpness of it in the room. Neuroscientist Candace Pert discovered the "molecules of emotion." biochemical messengers that circulate throughout the body. This means a parent's emotions are not just felt in their own mind, but transmitted chemically and energetically in ways their baby can sense.

A toddler may not grasp the phrase "*I love you*," but they sense the presence of it in a parent's energy.

In this stage, thoughts are not assembled as sentences. They arise as images, sensations, and symbolic associations. A child may feel hunger and visualize their favorite food. They may want attention and project an emotional pull toward the person they desire. When no one responds to their telepathic request, they may resort to crying. *Not* because crying is the first option, but because the subtler messages went unheard.

Clarifying Telepathy

Telepathy in this context refers to a spectrum of nonverbal communication that includes energetic transmission, emotional resonance, and sometimes a form of shared consciousness or mind-to-mind knowing. It is not science fiction; it is the natural, preverbal language of infants and toddlers, especially before filters of logic, skepticism, and social conditioning take hold. Psychologist Daniel Siegel has noted how "*mindsight*," the brain's ability to sense internal states and emotional attunement, is active in infants long before language appears. What modern science calls attunement, ancient wisdom calls soul connection.

Cultural Memory and Indigenous Understanding

Across cultures and history, preverbal communication has not always been suppressed. In many Indigenous traditions, children are understood to be spiritually open and energetically aware. Among the Kogi people of Colombia, babies are kept in dark, silent caves for their first year to preserve their inner vision. In Hawaiian Huna and Australian Aboriginal cultures, it is accepted that young children communicate telepathically with nature and the spirit world. These cultures never required children to "unlearn" the symbolic, intuitive language of the soul.

Contrast this with modern educational systems, which often train intuition out of children through rigid speech expectations, standardized testing, and dismissive attitudes toward imagination or emotional insight. The emphasis on verbal accuracy too early can create a fracture between what a child knows and what they are allowed to express.

Thinking in Symbols and Sensations

Children under the age of five do not think in complex words or sentences. Their internal world is a theater of symbols, body feelings, and sensory echoes. They experience memory as smell, mood, color, and vibration. The image of a red ball, the sound of a mother's laugh, the rhythm of being rocked to sleep: these are their mental landmarks.

This symbolic, sensory-based cognition is far closer to how dreams unfold than how adult thinking works. In fact, many researchers have likened early childhood consciousness to a dreamlike state, where everything is interconnected, layered, and emotional. This is not immaturity: it is a form of expanded perception.

The child does not yet separate the inner from the outer world. A thought and a feeling are the same thing. A wish and a reality are often interchangeable. And most notably, their minds are still open to receiving impressions from others without filtering them through skepticism or language.

How Language Reshapes the Mind

When verbal language begins to dominate, everything changes. Language is a tool; a magnificent one, but it is also a limiter. It defines. It separates. It puts experience into boxes.

As children begin to speak, their brains reorganize to favor logic, structure, and categorization. The fluid, intuitive awareness that allowed them to sense others' thoughts or feel their surroundings begins to narrow. Now, the question becomes, *"What word fits this feeling?"* rather than, *"What does this feeling communicate on its own?"*

This narrowing is reinforced by adults. We reward clear speech. We correct grammar. We celebrate vocabulary. In doing so, we often, unintentionally, suppress the deeper, more holistic language the child was already using.

Imagine when a child points to someone and says, "She's sad," you quickly teach by saying it is rude to point instead of first considering the message and the natural perceptions of the child. You might dismiss this unprompted insight as *imagination*. In moments like this, we subtly ask the child to mistrust or suppress the direct knowing they accessed so naturally.

The Role of Telepathy in Preverbal Life

In the earliest months and years, children often use telepathy not as an extra sense, but as a primary communication tool. When they want something, they may project that desire energetically before crying or gesturing. If the adults around them are attuned to their baby's thoughts, the baby is often met with what they need before they ever cry.

But in many cases, the adults are not listening telepathically. The child sends out an energetic request: "I'm hungry," or "I'm scared," and no one responds. Only then does the child cry.

Not as the first attempt at communication, but as the last.

Some children attempt to maintain this level of communication by using others as translators. A toddler might tug on their mother's arm and say, "Sissy wants her blanket," before the baby even stirs. Children often seem to "speak for" others before the others can speak for themselves. This is not precociousness. It is telepathy.

Understanding that children think in symbols and communicate telepathically changes everything about how we relate to them. It allows us to:

- Respond more to tone and feeling than to words.
- Watch for images, drawings, and behaviors as expressions of inner truth.
- Create environments that nourish intuitive connection.
- Treat crying not as manipulation, but as a signal that deeper messages were missed.

It also invites us, as adults, to return to our own preverbal knowing—to listen beyond the words, to feel the field, and to recognize that just because a child cannot yet speak does not mean they are not speaking volumes.

They are speaking with their eyes.

They are speaking with their hands.

They are speaking through their drawings.

They are speaking through their presence.

And often, they are speaking with their thoughts.

They still live in the wide and soft world of symbols and sensation. A world we once knew too, and can remember, if we allow ourselves to hear what is not said aloud.

Healing the Inner Child

For many adults, the key to healing deep emotional wounds lies not in retelling the story but in returning to the preverbal terrain where the story first took root. When we reconnect to image, sensation, sound, and feeling, without needing to name them, we open doors to memory and energy that words often obscure.

Therapists such as Gabor Maté have shown how early, nonverbal trauma is stored in the body and must be accessed *somatically* to be fully released. In this light, restoring the preverbal mind is not regression; it is transformation.

Science Note

Here are some important points in our understanding:

Dr. Bruce Lipton's work in *The Biology of Belief* shows that our perceptions—not just our genes—shape our biology. Our beliefs impact how cells behave, including what we notice or tune out.

Developmental researcher Joseph Chilton Pearce emphasized that play and imagination are biological necessities in early childhood, providing a developmental bridge between emotion and intellect.

Neuroscientist Dr. Candace Pert discovered neuropeptides, the *molecules of emotion*, demonstrating that emotions are biochemical messengers throughout the body, not just thoughts in the mind.

Psychiatrist Dr. Daniel Siegel adds that *mindsight*, the brain's ability to sense internal states and emotional resonance, is active in infants long before words.

Physician Dr. Gabor Maté has shown that early preverbal trauma is stored in the body and must be accessed through sensation and feeling rather than language.

Together, their research supports the idea that children perceive and respond to energy and emotion before they ever use words.

Practitioner Prompt

Encourage parents, educators, or caregivers to observe a child for one full day without relying on spoken instructions or questions. Instead, invite them to "tune in" to the child's energy, emotions, gestures, and silent cues.

Have them journal answers to the following:

1. What did I notice when I listened without words?
2. How did the child respond when I responded with presence instead of speech?
3. Did symbolic or emotional understanding feel stronger than verbal accuracy?
4. Use these notes in your next session to reflect on how the child's symbolic and telepathic language is still active; and how honoring it can strengthen connection.

Telepathy Toolbox

Let's play with energy! These activities help families become more aware of the unseen fields that connect us and the beautiful ways children mirror our emotions, thoughts, and presence.

Mirror Me with No Words

This practice strengthens nonverbal resonance and builds body-based empathy.

How to do it:

1. One person becomes the *Leader* and begins to move slowly: stretching, reaching, swaying.
2. The other person mirrors their movements without speaking.
3. Continue for one minute, then switch roles.
4. Reflect together afterward: *"How did it feel to lead? How did it feel to follow?"*

Why it works:

Mirroring bypasses language and highlights energetic attunement. Children quickly realize they can "feel" another's intention through movement, not just through words.

Feel My Field

This activity teaches children to sense and respect subtle energetic boundaries.

How to do it:

1. One person stands still with eyes closed.
2. The other person walks toward them slowly, one step at a time.
3. The first person raises their hand when they feel the other enter their energetic space, without opening their eyes.
4. Switch roles. (You can also try this with pets!)

Why it works:

Our nervous systems are wired to register the presence of others before words or touch. This practice validates a child's sensitivity to energetic fields and shows them that their perceptions are real.

Color the Feeling

This practice helps children translate energy into symbolic and visual expression.

How to do it:

1. Sit together and silently think of a strong feeling (peace, excitement, love).
2. Each person draws a picture using only colors, shapes, or patterns that match the feeling—rather than drawing a literal scene.
3. Share and guess each other's emotions.

Why it works:

Feelings carry frequency that often translates better into image and color than into words. Children gain confidence in expressing emotions symbolically, while parents learn to "read" their child's inner world.

Toolbox Wrap-Up

These playful practices show children that energy is real, visible, and shareable. By moving, sensing, and coloring together, families learn that connection happens in many forms beyond speech. The more you explore these invisible fields, the more you will discover that telepathy is not a trick to learn; it is a language you already share.

Invitation

Speak the Language of the Soul

This book is not just a manual of ideas. It is a map back to a truth you already know. The telepathic child is not just your student, your patient, or your own son or daughter. They are your mirror.

When you slow down, soften, and listen to the language beneath the language, you will find them waiting.

You will find yourself waiting too.

Transmission from the Telepathic Ones

We never left.

We wait in the silence between your thoughts.

In the child's whisper.

In the knowing glance.

In your dreams.

You knew us before language.

And now, you are beginning to hear us again.

Trust the remembering.

Up Next

After exploring the preverbal mind and how children think in symbols and sensations, we now turn to what happens when those early messages go unheard and how telepathy begins to fade when the world stops listening.

CHAPTER 3

Energy Fields and Morphic Resonance

We are more than biology.

Surrounding every human being is an energy field. It is a subtle, electromagnetic aura that holds our emotions, intentions, memories, and even our unspoken thoughts. This field, often imperceptible to the physical eye, is where the deeper language of telepathy lives. For children, especially in the early years, this energetic field is wide open, vibrant, and deeply attuned to the world around the child.

Understanding this unseen dimension is key to recognizing how children communicate, connect, and "just know" things. From heart fields to mirror neurons to morphic resonance, the science of subtle energy is rapidly catching up to what mothers, mystics, and intuitive teachers have known for generations: we are all connected, and energy is the language of that connection.

The Human Energy Field

Every person emits an energy field. Often called the aura, this field surrounds the body in multiple layers: physical, emotional, mental, and spiritual. These fields are in constant communication with the environment and with other beings. When someone walks into a room and you "feel their energy," you are responding to their aura.

The heart also has its own field. The HeartMath Institute has demonstrated that the human heart emits an electromagnetic field that can be detected up to three feet away from the body, and even further in sensitive environments. This field reflects our emotional state and can influence those around us. When a mother holds her infant, their heart fields synchronize. This synchronization helps regulate the baby's emotions, breathing, and nervous system.

In infancy and early childhood, a child's energy field is soft, expansive, and deeply receptive. They have not yet formed rigid boundaries or filters. They receive information through their auric field, like a radio tuned to all channels. When a parent is calm, the child relaxes. When a parent is anxious, the child may cry, fidget, or withdraw. These are not learned responses; they are energetic reflections.

Mirror Neurons: Feeling What Others Feel

Discovered in the early 1990s, mirror neurons are brain cells that fire both when an individual performs an action and when they observe someone else performing that same action. In other words, your brain responds as if you are doing the thing you are watching. These neurons are key to empathy, imitation, and social learning.

For children, mirror neurons play a major role in development. A toddler watches their parent laugh and feels joy. A baby sees another baby cry, and their own tears begin to flow. They are not mimicking deliberately. Their brains and energy fields are wired to resonate with the experience of others.

This is one reason children can become overwhelmed in chaotic environments or agitated when adults are silently upset. They are not being difficult. They are absorbing and reflecting the nervous systems of those around them. Mirror neurons allow for deep attunement, but also vulnerability.

Morphic Resonance and Collective Memory

British biologist Rupert Sheldrake proposed a controversial but intriguing theory called *morphic resonance*. He suggested that there exists a collective memory field shared by all members of a species. When one individual learns something, it becomes easier for others to learn it, even across space and time.

This helps explains phenomena such as why flocks of birds or schools of fish move in perfect harmony, or why scientific breakthroughs sometimes happen simultaneously across the globe. According to

Sheldrake, the more a pattern is repeated, the stronger the morphic field becomes.

Children tap into this field naturally. It helps explain how toddlers learn complex skills, like walking or language without explicit instruction. It may also explain why children born into spiritual or intuitive families retain telepathic abilities longer; they are immersed in a morphic field that supports energetic awareness.

The idea of morphic resonance aligns beautifully with the concept of telepathy. If thoughts and behaviors create fields that others can tap into, then communication does not require direct teaching; it requires attunement.

Cleve Backster and the Consciousness of Life

Another well-known contributor to the field of energetic communication was Cleve Backster, a polygraph expert who, in the 1960s, discovered what became known as *The Backster Effect*. He connected a polygraph machine to a houseplant and, on a whim, imagined burning one of its leaves. To his astonishment, the polygraph indicated the plant was in distress.

He repeated similar experiments with plants, yogurt cultures, and even human cells separated from the body. The conclusion? Living organisms respond to thoughts and intentions, even from a distance.

Backster's work, though dismissed by mainstream science, offers powerful support for telepathic and energetic connection. It reinforces what many mothers already know:

- A plant droops when the person who nurtures it leaves the house.
- A pet becomes distressed when their human is about to go on a trip.
- A mother feels a "jolt" the moment her child is injured, even if miles away.

These responses occur faster than any physical signal can travel. They are examples of instantaneous energetic communication.

The Soul Cord: Energetic Link Between Parent and Child

Beyond the scientific, there is a metaphysical truth: the connection between parent and child is more than physical. It is soul-deep. Many intuitive traditions speak of a *soul cord,* often called the *silver cord* that links parents and children, especially mothers and infants.

This *soul cord* allows for a constant exchange of emotional and energetic information. It is why mothers often wake just before their baby cries, even in another room. It is why a father might feel dread moments before a distant child is hurt. These moments are not coincidence; they are echoes traveling along the *soul cord.*

As the child grows, this cord remains, though it may stretch or shift in expression. Some parents still feel their *teenager's emotions* from afar. Others sense when their adult children are struggling, even without contact. This is not guesswork. It is the enduring vibrational bond formed through love and shared experience.

Vibrational Attunement and Family Fields

Every family operates within a shared vibrational field. This field holds collective emotions, beliefs, and energetic patterns. Children are especially attuned to the frequency of this field and often serve as reflectors of its health.

When the family is calm, the child thrives. When the family is stressed or emotionally congested, the child may act out, become sick, or withdraw. The child is not the problem; they are the indicator.

This vibrational field also means that healing one member of the family can raise the vibration of the entire system. When a parent begins meditation, emotional work, or energy healing, the child often improves as well, even without direct involvement. The fields are linked. A change in one member shifts the whole.

Now that we've seen how children live in a world of feeling and frequency, we turn our attention to the science and metaphysics behind that sensitivity. Understanding energy fields, mirror neurons, and morphic resonance changes how we relate to children.

It allows us to:

- Respect their sensitivity as a sign of deep attunement, not weakness.
- Create environments that support energetic coherence.
- Recognize that our inner state affects our children more than our words do.
- Restore faith in the nonverbal, intuitive bonds that make parenting so sacred.

This growing field is supported by pioneers such as Daniel J Siegel, MD, whose work on nervous system co-regulation and the *felt sense* gives language to the emotional resonance between parent and child; Dr. Candace Pert, whose discovery of the *molecules of emotion* reveals how feelings are both biochemical and vibrational; and Lynne McTaggart, whose research in *The Field* uncovers the power of group consciousness and intention. These perspectives converge to affirm that what we feel, think, and project matters, not just chemically, but energetically.

It also calls us to a higher level of awareness. *Children are reading us all the time.* They are not just reading our behavior. They are reading our energy. They are receivers and amplifiers of the field around them.

The Goldmans and Vibrational Coherence

Jonathan and Andi Goldman's research on sound and resonance adds an essential dimension to our understanding of energetic communication. Their award-winning work, The Humming Effect, demonstrates how simple humming can create measurable shifts in the body's physiology and field by increasing nitric oxide, strengthening vagal tone, calming the nervous system, and supporting the heart–brain connection that underlies intuitive awareness.

Sound is not just heard; it is felt as vibration throughout the body and into the surrounding field. Children are naturally attuned to energy patterns that extend beyond spoken language. When people hum, they generate a coherent vibrational signal that others can sense. Psychoacoustic research confirms that harmonic tones help regulate emotion, entrain brainwaves, and create shared resonance between people.

Integrating the Goldman's findings with broader field theories suggests sound is one of the most accessible gateways into nonlocal connection, which helps explain why many telepathy games involving humming are so effective. Sound organizes energy—and children instinctively use it to communicate, regulate, and connect.

Science Note

Modern research in neuroscience and field theory supports the possibility that consciousness and memory can be nonlocal. The HeartMath Institute has demonstrated that heart rhythms can synchronize between individuals, supporting emotional connection. Rupert Sheldrake's studies on morphic resonance suggest that memory and behavior are shared across fields of experience, helping explain why children often *just know*. The Goldman's research on sound and resonance adds an essential dimension to our understanding of energetic communication

Cleve Backster's experiments with plants and even isolated cells indicated that living systems respond to human thoughts and emotions, even at a distance. Psychiatrist Daniel Siegel's work in interpersonal neurobiology shows how nervous systems co-regulate, confirming that children mirror the internal states of caregivers. Candace Pert's research also demonstrated that these emotional molecules do not just stay in the brain, they travel through the entire body and interact with receptors in every system. This supports the idea that emotion is not localized thought but a full-body field, one that children can sense and respond to.

Lynne McTaggart's research in *The Field* documents how group consciousness and intention can influence people and the environment.

Jonathan and Andi Goldman's work in The Humming Effect shows that humming creates measurable coherence in the body's electromagnetic and nervous systems. Their research demonstrates that simple vocal toning increases nitric oxide, supports heart–brain synchronization, and generates a stable vibrational field that others can feel. Because sound carries intention, humming becomes a direct pathway into energetic connection. This helps explain why children instinctively hum to regulate themselves and to attune to those around them.

Together, these findings affirm that what children perceive is not limited to what is spoken; they are tuning into the world around them.

Practitioner Prompt

Ask the caregiver or parent to pause each evening and reflect: "What did I project into the field today?" Invite them to journal for one week noting how the child responded to their emotional or energetic state. Then suggest a grounding practice, like breathwork or heart-focused meditation, before interactions with the child. Track if increased coherence in the parent corresponds with increased ease in the child.

Telepathy is not magic. It is biology meeting spirit. It is what happens when open hearts share frequency across space, without the need for sound. And it begins not with something we teach our children, but with something we remember together.

As we learn to become conscious stewards of our own energy fields, we begin to mirror the same attunement and coherence we wish to cultivate in our children. Their healing often begins with our own.

In the dance of energy, every thought is a signal. Every feeling, a frequency. Every bond, a channel of light.

And our children? They are listening to all of it.

Telepathy Toolbox

These practices are not about performance; they are about play. Each one invites children to notice energy, trust their sensations, and discover that what they feel inside is already a form of communication.

Let's play with energy! These activities help families become more aware of the unseen fields that connect us and the beautiful ways children mirror our emotions, thoughts, and presence.

Feel It First

Invite your baby or toddler to communicate through emotion before words.

How to do it:

1. Pause before responding to your child.
2. Close your eyes for one slow breath.
3. Sense into their emotional field and silently ask, *What are you trying to tell me?*
4. · Notice any feeling, color, or sensation that arises in your body.
5. · Respond gently based on the emotion you "read."
6. · Keep the moment short, warm, and grounded.

Why it works:

Children broadcast emotional information energetically before they can speak. When you attune to their field, you model intuitive listening and strengthen their natural telepathic channels.

Sound and Soothe

Use tone instead of words to connect with your child's emotional state.

How to do it:

1. Sit close so your child can feel the vibration of your voice.
2. Begin humming softly or singing wordless tones.

3. Match the emotion you sense (slow for sad, bright for playful).
4. Gradually shift your tone toward calm and comfort.
5. ·Notice how your child's breathing and posture change.
6. ·End when your child settles or shifts emotionally.

Why it works:

Babies interpret vibration long before language. Tones regulate the nervous system and create a shared emotional frequency you both feel.

Symbol Basket

Help children communicate inner stories using objects instead of words.

How to do it:

1. Fill a small basket with simple items such as feathers, stones, shells, and fabric squares.
2. Sit with your child in a quiet space.
3. Invite them to "show you a story" using only objects.
4. · Watch how they place, stack, sort, or sequence the items.
5. · Ask gentle questions such as, "What does this one feel like?"
6. · Mirror their choices with curiosity, not interpretation.

Why it works:

Object-based storytelling taps into symbolic thinking, an early form of intuitive and telepathic expression. Children reveal emotions more easily through play than verbal explanation.

Image Sharing

Practice sending and receiving silent pictures together.

How to do it:

1. Sit facing each other with relaxed bodies.
2. Choose a simple image in your mind (tree, apple, rainbow).
3. Hold the image for three breaths before "sending" it.

4. · Have your child draw what comes to mind without overthinking.
5. · Compare drawings after each round.
6. · Switch roles once or twice to keep it playful.

Why it works:

Quiet visualization builds the mental-image muscles used in telepathic communication. Children often receive symbolic impressions faster than adults expect.

Dreamtime Drawing

Turn early-morning dream energy into intuitive expression.

How to do it:

1. Keep crayons or pencils ready by the bedside.
2. Upon waking, draw together without speaking.
3. Let colors and shapes flow freely.
4. · Share feelings or images after the drawing is complete.
5. · Notice repeated symbols or emotions over time.
6. · Keep drawings in a small dream journal if desired.

Why it works:

The brain transitions through theta state upon waking, a prime frequency for intuition. Drawing in silence helps children express nonverbal impressions carried over from dreams.

Tone Tracking

Let sound guide a child into deeper sensory and emotional awareness.

How to do it:

1. Play soft music, sound bowls, chimes, or nature tones.
2. Invite your child to move, sway, or draw as they listen.
3. Ask afterward, "What did the sound feel like?"
4. Offer descriptive feeling words if they need help.

5. ·Try different sound types to explore contrasts.

6. ·Keep sessions short to preserve fascination.

Why it works:

Sound bypasses logic and goes straight to the intuitive centers of the brain. Children naturally translate vibration into movement, color, and emotion—a foundation for telepathic sensing.

Toolbox Wrap-Up

These playful practices show children that energy is real, visible, and shareable. By moving, sensing, and coloring together, families learn that connection happens in many forms beyond speech. The more you explore these invisible fields, the more you will discover that telepathy is not a trick to learn; it is a language you already share.

Invitation

You are not just raising a child. You are shaping a field.

Every thought, every glance, every unspoken feeling becomes part of the invisible web you share.

This chapter has revealed what ancient wisdom and modern science now agree on: energy speaks louder than words. Mirror neurons, heart fields, morphic resonance, and soul cords remind us that connection is not taught; it is remembered.

So, take a moment today. Breathe. Center. Notice what you are radiating.

Your child is not just listening with their ears.

They are listening with their entire being.

Let your energy say what your words cannot.

In that silent space between you, a sacred language is born.

Let's explore what happens when these subtle conversations awaken memory, emotion, and even past lives.

Transmission from the Telepathic Ones

We speak in waves, not words.

We read your heart before your hands.

In the language of light, you are fluent; you just forgot.

Breathe. Feel. Project love.

And you will hear us again.

Up Next

As we begin to understand the energetic bonds that shape our children's inner world, we must now ask, "What stories are they carrying that did not begin in this lifetime?"

CHAPTER 4

How We Shut It Down

After exploring how children attune to the nature of subtle energies, we must now look honestly at what happens when those channels begin to close, not out of malice, but through modern life. Children arrive in this world with their energetic channels wide open. They are deeply attuned to emotion, intention, and subtle frequencies. They communicate telepathically through images, feelings, and unspoken knowing. All too often, this natural gift is shut down, not maliciously, but through social norms, education systems, cultural conditioning, and even well-meaning adults.

When the World Says "Do Not See That"

One of the earliest forms of suppression happens when a child "*sees*" something others do not see and is corrected or dismissed. A child may say, "There's a man in the hallway," or "My angel told me not to go," and the adult replies, "There's nothing there. Do not be silly." These phrases are often delivered with the intent to comfort or protect, but they have a different effect entirely.

I met a young girl, about seven or nine years old, at an expo. She asked if I could see the black cat perched near the ceiling in the corner of the room we were in. I told her that I could not. She looked at me seriously and said, "Do you believe me?" I said, "Sure." She nodded quietly and said, "My mom told me there is no such thing and to stop talking about it." In that moment, I could see the heartbreak of being unseen, and her quiet courage in still asking.

Children quickly learn that some things are acceptable to talk about, and some are not. When their intuitive insights, visions, or feelings are repeatedly invalidated, they begin to question themselves. The message becomes clear: "Do not trust what you sense. Only believe what others sense, too."

As this continues, the child begins to filter out their natural awareness. They do not lose the ability. It just goes dormant and gets buried under years of trying to fit in and "be normal."

Talking Right Over Sensing

In our society, *language is king*. From early on, children are praised for speaking clearly, reading early, and using big words. We test, measure, and celebrate verbal milestones while often ignoring intuitive ones.

This emphasis on speaking correctly over sensing intuitively teaches children to value words more than sensations. A child might know something energetically but hesitate to express it unless they can verbalize it perfectly. Slowly, the quiet knowing is replaced by the need to explain, label, and justify.

Instead of asking, *"What do you feel in your body?"* or *"Did anything pop into your mind just now?"* we ask, *"What did the book say?"* or *"Can you say that better?"* The intuitive becomes secondary to the articulate. And so, the telepathic channel begins to close, not through force, but through emphasis.

The Imagination Trap

How many times has a child said something remarkable, only to be met with, *"That's just your imagination."*? While imagination is often praised in play, it is often used as a brush-off when children speak truths that feel uncomfortable or unprovable.

Imagination and intuition exist on the same frequency. When a child shares an impression, vision, or insight, it may come through the imagination, but that does not make it untrue. It makes it symbolic, energetic, and worthy of exploration.

When we teach children that imagination is separate from truth, we disconnect them from one of their greatest sources of intuitive knowing. We teach them that unless something is physical and provable, it is not

44

real. And yet, some of the most accurate insights like dreams, gut feelings, and inner pictures, come through the very pathways we label as fantasy.

Screens, Stimulation, and the Loss of Presence

Another factor in the diminishing of telepathic ability is overstimulation. Today's children are surrounded by televisions, tablets, phones, videos, and games, all of which keep their attention externally focused and constantly shifting.

While some technology can be used for conscious learning, most digital content disrupts the stillness needed for subtle sensing. Telepathy thrives in quiet, simplicity, and focused presence. A child in constant motion, absorbing flashing images and rapid-fire noise, is not in a state where energetic communication can flourish.

Presence is the foundation of telepathy. It requires tuning in, not zoning out. But modern culture rewards distraction. Children are entertained to keep them quiet, rather than encouraged to explore their inner world.

There's Another Layer:
EMFs (Electromagnetic Frequencies)

The growing brain of a child is especially vulnerable to electromagnetic fields (EMFs), emitted by Wi-Fi, cell phones, routers, smart devices, and more. *EMFs* interfere with the body's natural electrical field. For intuitive children, this disruption can cloud their clarity, affect their sleep, distort their mood, and even suppress their inner knowing. The more we surround children with unfiltered electromagnetic noise, the more we risk muting their natural sensitivity.

These modern-day stressors also interfere with the *biofield*, diminishing a child's natural ability to tune in and perceive energetically.

Research supports these concerns. Dr. Dietrich Klinghardt has shown that EMFs can disrupt the pineal gland, the nervous system, and the body's regulatory system. The effects are especially pronounced in sensitive children. Similarly, Dr. David O. Carpenter, a public health physician, has warned about children's heightened vulnerability to EMFs and other neurotoxic environmental exposures. Together, their work underscores the profound risks EMFs pose to developing bodies and intuitive awareness.

School Systems and Conformity

Education is often where telepathy is finally buried. School systems are structured to reward logic, conformity, and measurable outcomes. Children are taught to follow instructions, stay on task, and speak when called on.

Creative, intuitive, or nonlinear thinking is often labeled as daydreaming or distraction. Children who "know" things but cannot explain how, are told they need to "show their work."

Feelings are not typically part of the curriculum, and telepathic communication certainly is not.

Sensitive children may be overwhelmed by the group energy of a classroom, absorbing the feelings of their peers. But instead of being supported in grounding and clearing their field, they may be labeled as hyperactive, withdrawn, or disruptive.

And so, through a thousand small adjustments, like "Sit still." "Pay attention." "Stop making things up." "Prove it." "Get your head out of the clouds." the child separates from their amazing intuitive self.

Reclaiming What Was Lost

The good news is this: telepathy never disappears. It simply waits. Beneath the layers of training and filtering, the original connection still exists.

Many adults begin to reclaim their intuitive abilities later in life through parenting, crisis, spiritual awakening, or intentional practice. And children who are supported, validated, and protected can retain their gifts well beyond early childhood.

To help children hold on to their intuitive power, we must create space for their inner experiences. We must ask what they sense, not just what they know. We must validate their feelings, their pictures, their gut responses. And we must protect their environments from overstimulation, emotional suppression, EMFs, and even fluoridated water.

Most of all, we must listen. Truly listen, to what they say, and to what they do not.

Because sometimes, what they do not say is the message they most want us to receive.

Fluoride and the Pineal Gland

A growing body of research supports the biological basis of intuitive awareness in children. The HeartMath Institute has demonstrated that emotional coherence improves intuition and decision-making.

Fluoride's impact on the pineal gland is also documented in neuroscience literature, suggesting it may impair melatonin production and calcify tissues associated with inner perception.

One of the most critical physical contributors to the suppression of intuitive ability is fluoride exposure. Fluoride, commonly found in tap water and dental products, has been shown to calcify the pineal gland: a tiny endocrine gland in the center of the brain long associated with spiritual perception, dream recall, and higher consciousness.

The pineal gland is sometimes called the *"seat of the soul"* and is believed to play a central role in telepathy, visualization, and energetic communication. In children, the pineal gland is especially active. However, over time, excessive fluoride exposure may inhibit its function.

Thinkers such as Dr. Joe Dispenza and Dr. Bruce Lipton have emphasized that the pineal gland is more than a physical structure. They describe it as a kind of inner antenna, a bridge between biology and consciousness, that allows us to tune into wider fields of perception.

As the pineal gland calcifies, so does intuitive clarity. Dreams become dull, inner imagery fades, and spontaneous knowing becomes less accessible. Protecting the pineal gland means preserving the gateway through which many children access their telepathic gifts.

Science Note

There are multiple contributors to pineal suppression, including excessive calcium supplements, chlorine in drinking water, heavy metals such as mercury and aluminum, and artificial additives commonly found in processed foods. These substances may accumulate in the body and disrupt natural energetic and hormonal systems. Even limited exposure in early childhood can produce significant long-term effects on the developing pineal gland (see Appendix F: Broad Spectrum DeTOX). Encouraging natural light exposure, clean water, a whole-foods diet, and mindful detoxification practices can help preserve this vital center of perception.

Research from the HeartMath Institute demonstrates that emotional coherence strengthens intuitive accuracy and decision-making, showing that heart-based states directly influence perception. Dr. Dietrich Klinghardt's clinical research suggests that EMFs disrupt the pineal gland and nervous system, weakening the body's natural energetic balance. Dr. David O. Carpenter has warned that children's developing brains are especially vulnerable to EMFs and other environmental toxins, which may further suppress intuitive clarity.

As Dr. Joe Dispenza and Dr. Bruce Lipton have both described, the pineal gland may function as a kind of quantum antenna; an inner organ of perception that connects the body to its energy field. When this is muted or distorted, the ability to intuit, perceive symbolically, or receive higher insight becomes significantly diminished.

Invite caregivers to reflect: "When did I first stop trusting my intuition?" Then ask them to observe one day of their child's spontaneous comments or 'odd' perceptions with curiosity, and without correction. Create a "Telepathy Journal" together for one week. Afterward, review the entries together. This creates a safe space for the child to keep their intuitive channels open and teaches the adult to listen without filtering.

Telepathy Toolbox

These gentle family activities reopen intuitive channels that may have closed over time, whether from busyness, doubt, or dismissal. Treat them as playful invitations back to presence, not pressured practices.

Draw the Dream That Did Not Get Shared

Invite family members to express inner imagery they've kept to themselves.

How to do it:
1. Before bed, ask each person to think of a dream or inner image they've never talked about.
2. The next morning, everyone draws or colors that "forgotten" dream—even if it is just a shape or feeling.
3. Share drawings only if it feels safe.

Why it works:

Dreams and inner images are forms of telepathic memory. Honoring them, even in private, validates that unspoken experiences matter and can be expressed without judgment.

What Was Not Said

Explore the feelings that remain beneath unspoken words.

How to do it:

1. Recall a moment in your day that felt "off" or incomplete, when no one spoke about it.
2. Sit in a circle. Each person silently draws what they think another person was feeling in that moment.
3. Share drawings and reflect together.

Why it works:

Children often sense the unsaid. This practice shows them their impressions are valid, while helping families recognize the depth of silent communication.

The Unseen Friend Game

Honor the presence of "imaginary" companions as messengers of truth.

How to do it:

1. Invite each child or adult to describe an "imaginary" friend they had—or one they wish they had.
2. Ask gentle questions: *What did they look like? What did they tell you? How did they make you feel?*
3. Listen without correction, and celebrate the stories shared.

Why it works:

So-called "imaginary" friends often represent guides, inner voices, or symbolic truths. Valuing them affirms children's unseen worlds instead of dismissing them.

Float the Feeling

Translate wordless emotions into symbols and images.

How to do it:

1. Each person writes down or scribbles a wordless feeling on a slip of paper (color or symbol).
2. Fold the papers and place them in a bowl of water.
3. Let them float briefly, then take turns drawing one.

4. Guess what the energy felt like, then draw how it looked inside.

Why it works:

This activity transforms emotions into symbols. By expressing feelings as colors or shapes, children learn emotional literacy through play.

The Listening Candle

Use silence to attune to inner voices.

How to do it:

1. Light a single candle in the center of the group.
2. Sit together in silence for one minute, gazing softly at the flame.
3. Afterward, each person shares what they "heard" inside themselves.

Why it works:

The candle creates a sacred pause where inner impressions can surface. Children discover that silence is not empty—it is full of subtle messages and presence.

Toolbox Wrap-Up

These activities remind families that what is unspoken still communicates. Whether through dreams, drawings, or silence, children reveal their inner language when given space to share. By honoring what was not said, you keep intuitive channels open and teach that the unseen world is just as real—and valuable—as the spoken one.

These gentle family activities help reopen intuitive channels that may have closed over time—whether from busyness, doubt, or dismissal. Treat them as playful invitations back to presence, not pressured practices.

Invitation

Even if the world once asked you to forget, you can choose now to remember your child's whispers, their drawings, their quiet pauses. They are still speaking the soul's first language.

Each time you respond with wonder instead of correction, you rebuild the bridge back to the sacred.

And each time you honor the unseen, the unheard, and the unspoken, you begin to heal not just your child's trust, but your own.

Transmission from the Telepathic Ones

You were never meant to close the door, but you did, because the world asked you to. We have kept the light burning inside your dreams. The child still remembers, and so do you.

Breathe. Feel. Listen. You will hear us in the spaces between again.

Up Next

As we begin the next chapter, we will explore how this suppression can be reversed, how listening can be relearned, and how to reawaken connections. What does it take to reclaim this inner guidance? Let's find out.

CHAPTER 5

Signs Your Child is Using Telepathy

Telepathy is not a skill that only a rare few children possess. It is the natural language of all children before words take hold, and for many, it lingers much longer than we realize. Some children retain telepathy into their school years, while others never lose it. The golden key is recognizing the signs.

Telepathic communication does not always appear in mystical or dramatic ways. It often shows up in everyday moments: a knowing glance, a perfectly timed sentence, an emotional reaction that seems to come from nowhere. The more we understand these behaviors, the more we can support and nurture the silent gift within them.

Observable Behaviors and Intuitive Reactions

You might notice that your child responds to your thoughts or emotions before you say anything aloud. They may turn to look at you just as you are about to speak, or shift their behavior before you ask them to. These are signs of energetic awareness.

Other common signs include:

- Sudden mood changes that match the feelings of people around them
- Laughing or crying in sync with others, even from a distance
- Avoiding certain people without clear explanation
- Becoming overwhelmed in crowds or noisy environments due to energetic overload

Children who are still using telepathy often react strongly to energy, not just words. If you are thinking about leaving the house, they might ask, "Where are you going?" before you have moved. If you are sad but hiding it, they may become clingy, angry, or withdrawn. They feel what you feel, whether or not you have spoken it aloud.

Finishing Sentences, Reading Moods, and *Just Knowing*

Some children consistently finish your sentences or answer questions before you have asked them. Others seem to "read the room" instantly, shifting their behavior based on unspoken tensions or joys. These children may seem highly perceptive, even precocious, but what they are really doing is tuning into your energetic and emotional signals.

Telepathic children often:

- Know who is on the phone before it rings
- Speak a desire or idea that you were just thinking
- Act on instructions before you say them
- Express needs or insights that are beyond their verbal or developmental level

For example, a parent might be thinking, "We should go for a walk," when the child suddenly says, "Let's go outside!" Another child might tell a parent, "You are thinking about Grandma," even when nothing was said aloud. These moments are subtle but deeply significant. They are proof of a deeper channel of connection.

Some children also mirror their caregiver's inner world. If you are trying to hide worry, your child may act out that feeling in behavior: crying, fidgeting, or having a tantrum. They are not misbehaving; they are resonating with unspoken frequencies.

These observations align with the growing fields of interpersonal neurobiology and energetic resonance. Dr. Daniel Siegel refers to this deep brain-to-brain sensitivity as the *"felt sense,"* where one nervous system synchronizes with another.

The Institute of HeartMath Institute has also demonstrated that the electromagnetic field of the heart can create coherence between people, particularly between parents and children. And Dr. Rupert Sheldrake's concept of *morphic resonance* offers a broader understanding of how children can "just know" things that seem impossible to learn through traditional senses. They are tuning into a collective energetic field.

Stories from the Field

Countless parents have shared stories that confirm their children are still operating on an intuitive, telepathic wavelength.

Case 1 – A mother was quietly wrestling with whether to accept a new job offer. She had not spoken a word about it around her children; the decision was still turning silently in her mind. As she sat nearby, her five-year-old daughter looked up from coloring and, without hesitation, said, "I do not want you to leave your job yet. Your friends will be sad." The mother froze—her daughter had named the very reason she was hesitant: she loved her coworkers. This was not guesswork. It was a clear window into the mother's private thoughts, offered through the child's intuitive attunement.

Case 2 – One afternoon, a toddler began crying inconsolably. Nothing seemed to soothe him, and the timing felt odd—there was no obvious trigger. Ten minutes later, the father's phone rang: his own mother had just been in a car accident. Looking back, he realized the child's distress had coincided almost exactly with the moment of impact. This became one of those family stories no one could explain away. The child had felt the emotional ripple through the field of connection before anyone had spoken a word.

Case 3 – A boy with very limited verbal skills looked at the sky on a clear day and calmly announced, "It is going to snow tomorrow." His parents smiled, knowing that in their warm climate snowfall was nearly unheard of, and certainly not in the forecast. Yet the next morning, they awoke to find the ground dusted white from a rare snowstorm. The boy had not seen a weather report, and he could not articulate how he knew. He had simply tuned into a larger rhythm—an atmospheric "knowing" that bypassed language and logic.

Case 4 – During an ordinary afternoon, a three-year-old suddenly told his mom, "You do not have to be scared. The doctor said you are okay now." His mother had received good medical news that morning but had shared it with no one. In fact, she was still processing relief from the anxiety she'd carried for weeks. For her son to speak her private truth so clearly was both comforting and startling. She realized in that moment how open children can be to the emotional states and even unspoken relief of the adults around them.

Case 5 – At a family gathering, a young boy walked over to his cousin without saying a word and handed her a stuffed animal. Then he said softly, "You are sad because you miss your dog." His cousin burst into tears. Her dog had died that very morning, and she had not told anyone. The boy's gesture was not random, it was direct recognition of her grief, coupled with an act of comfort. In his intuitive awareness, he had not only received her silent sorrow but had responded with compassion.

These stories remind us that telepathy is not a rare phenomenon—it is woven into daily life. Children do not filter, doubt, or second-guess their impressions; they simply share what they feel. When we take them seriously, we see how naturally they remain attuned to the invisible threads of connection that bind us all.

A Parent's Checklist:
Is My Child Still Using Telepathy?

Here is a simple checklist to help parents identify signs of active telepathy in their child. While every child is different, answering "yes" to several of these questions may suggest that your child is still using their intuitive, energetic communication skills.

- Does your child often respond to your thoughts before you speak them?
- Do they finish your sentences or know what you are about to say?
- Have they ever told you something about someone else that they had no way of knowing?
- Do they show sudden emotional shifts in response to your internal state?
- Have they made accurate predictions about people, events, or weather?
- Do they react to certain people or places with no logical reason?
- Have they told you what someone else is thinking or feeling without being told?

- Do they seem to "know" who is calling or visiting before it happens?
- Do they act before you have given them instructions?
- Have they ever described dreams or images that matched someone else's?
- Are they sensitive to tone, body language, and subtle cues far beyond their age?
- Do they share information they could not have overheard or been taught?

If these behaviors are present, it is likely your child is still accessing their natural telepathic ability.

But also remember that not every intuitive child shows these signs overtly. Some communicate more internally, through dreams, symbolic art, silent knowing, or unspoken empathy. The absence of obvious signs does not mean absence of the gift. It may simply mean it is quiet, waiting, or expressed differently.

Learning Telepathy with Your Child

Once you recognize your child's telepathic gifts, you can begin nurturing them through playful, intentional connection. You do not have to be psychic or trained. You simply need to become quiet, curious, and receptive.

Encouraging the Gift

When you recognize the signs, affirm them. Let your child know that their awareness is real and valued. Avoid brushing off their insights as imagination or coincidence. Instead, respond with curiosity: *"How did you know that?"* or *"Tell me more about what you felt."*

Create an environment for natural energetic communication

Turn off background noise, allow moments of shared silence, and model presence. Children's telepathic gifts flourish in stillness.

If your child seems overwhelmed by energy, teach them simple grounding techniques: stomping feet, placing hands on the heart, or visualizing a golden light surrounding them. These tools will help them manage their sensitivity rather than shut it down.

And perhaps most importantly, trust your own intuition. The more you tune in to your own telepathic abilities, the easier it becomes to recognize and nurture them in your child. It becomes a shared language, one that transcends words.

Telepathy is not lost. It is simply waiting to be remembered, honored, and lived.

And our children are showing us how.

Science Note

Research from the HeartMath Institute shows that emotional coherence strengthens intuitive accuracy, a finding measured through heart rate variability and other physiological markers. Psychiatrist Daniel Siegel's work in interpersonal neurobiology demonstrates that children literally "feel" the nervous systems of those around them, synchronizing brain and body states in ways that shape emotional development. Biologist Rupert Sheldrake's theory of morphic fields, though debated, provide a powerful explanatory framework for the way children seem to tap into collective memory fields, accessing information in ways that appear instantaneous, and inexplicable through ordinary senses. Together, these perspectives reinforce that telepathy is not fantasy: it is biologically and energetically real.

Have caregivers create a Telepathy Journal for one week. Ask them to record moments when their child seems to know something without being told. At the end of the week, reflect:

- Were these just coincidences?
- Was there a pattern?

Awareness is the first key to providing support. Use the notes to adjust family practices next week.

Telepathy Toolbox

These simple practices help families and children reawaken the channel of silent knowing. Keep them playful, lighthearted, and short—telepathy grows best through curiosity, not pressure.

Eye-to-Eye Images

This exercise strengthens the telepathic bond through shared presence.

How to do it:

1. Sit with your child, in a calm space.
2. Look gently into each other's eyes and take 2–3 deep breaths together.
3. Close your eyes and silently imagine an object (apple, balloon, rainbow).
4. After a few seconds, ask your child what they "saw."
5. Accept any answer—do not push or correct.

Why it works:

Children are highly responsive to visual telepathy. Eye contact builds resonance, while imagery strengthens their confidence in what they perceive.

Silent Guessing Games

A fun way to practice intention and reception with numbers.

How to do it:

1. Think of a number between 1 and 5, holding it clearly in mind.
2. Ask your child to guess.
3. Celebrate every near match.
4. Gradually increase the number range as they get more comfortable.

Why it works:

Numbers give children a simple structure to test their intuitive impressions. Expanding the range builds trust in subtle messages without pressure to be "perfect."

Drawing Each Other's Thoughts

Turn telepathy into art and creativity.

How to do it:

1. Sit together with paper and colors.
2. Each person silently thinks of a color, shape, animal, or scene.
3. The other draws what comes to mind.
4. Compare drawings and notice overlaps.

Why it works:

Drawing bypasses logic and lets intuition flow symbolically. This reinforces that telepathic impressions can take many forms—colors, shapes, or images.

Bedtime Messages

Use the dream state as a bridge for telepathic communication.

How to do it:

1. As your child is falling asleep, silently hold a clear, loving intention.

2. Send them an image or phrase such as *"You are safe"* or *"I am proud of you."*

3. In the morning, ask if they remember any dreams, images, or feelings.

Why it works:

The relaxed state before sleep opens children's intuitive channels. Bedtime telepathy often surfaces in dreams, giving children confidence that love travels across states of awareness.

Family Telepathy Play

Include siblings, grandparents, and caregivers in the fun.

How to do it:

1. Invite siblings to try image-sharing or guessing games.

2. Create group activities: story circles, drawing what others are thinking, or scavenger hunts guided by silent cues.

3. Celebrate patterns and insights as a group.

Why it works:

Practicing as a family builds trust and strengthens emotional bonds. Shared play shows that telepathy is not rare—it is part of the family's natural language.

Honoring Insights

Normalize telepathy by acknowledging it out loud.

How to do it:

1. Use phrases like:

   - *"I wonder if you heard me thinking that."*

   - *"That is just what I was about to say! You are so connected."*

- *"You always seem to know when I am feeling something. Thank you for noticing."*

2. Say these in real moments when your child shows awareness.

Why it works:

Children's confidence grows when their intuitive insights are named and valued. They learn that their inner world is trustworthy and real.

Toolbox Wrap-Up

These activities weave telepathy into daily life with ease. By sending images, playing guessing games, or sharing drawings, you remind your child that their silent insights are valid. The more you honor and celebrate these moments, the more natural telepathy becomes—until it feels less like practice and more like the language you always shared.

Invitation

Your child's telepathic abilities are not fantasy or coincidence; they are truth, spoken in the soul's first language.

The more you validate what cannot be seen but is deeply felt, the more that channel of connection remains open.

Observe.
Listen.
Honor.

When you trust their knowing, you also rediscover your own.

Transmission from the Telepathic Ones

We are the ones who still hear the whispers.
We feel when you think of us, even without words.
You taught us words, but we remember the silence beneath them.
You are not separate. You never were.
We are listening. Always.
And we are waiting for you to remember.

Up Next

As we step into Chapter 6, we will explore how adults can reopen their own channels of perception.

Autism, Silence, and the Secret Language

In recent years, autism has become one of the most talked about developmental diagnoses and also one of the least understood. From a metaphysical perspective, autism may be seen less as a disorder and more as a unique pattern of wiring. This wiring may be one that preserves the child's access to higher frequencies, nonverbal communication, and telepathy.

Many autistic children are born without the usual "filters" that most of us develop. They do not interpret the world through the lens of social rules, sarcasm, or performance. They interact with energy as it is: pure, direct, and often overwhelming.

Reframe the Box

Conventional View of Autism:
Developmental delay or disorder
Language and social impairments
Behavioral management focus
Emphasis on normalization

Energetic/Metaphysical View:
Advanced sensory and energetic perception
Alternative communication pathways
Sacred divergence, not disorder
Anchors of crystalline consciousness

A Different Kind of Knowing

While some children on the autism spectrum may not speak, they often show deep understanding. They notice patterns that others miss. They remember conversations they never seemed to be part of. They anticipate needs, reactions, and emotions, sometimes without any logical explanation.

This is not accidental; autistic children often live closer to truth. Their sensitivities are not flaws; they are openings. Because they are not fully immersed in the *rules* of language and behavior, they may remain attuned to the energetic signals most people tune out.

One mother shared that her nonverbal son could "feel" who was about to visit before the doorbell rang. He would go to the window or prepare a toy for a specific person. Another child refused to go into certain rooms or buildings, seemingly reacting to energetic imprints long forgotten by others.

This echoes what Temple Grandin, one of the most well-known autistic voices, has described: heightened sensory awareness is not a dysfunction but a different form of perception. Dr. Stephen Porges' *Polyvagal Theory* supports this, explaining that what may appear as social withdrawal is often a nervous system response to overstimulation, not rejection. Dr. Bruce Lipton's work on epigenetics further reveals how environment and frequency influence cellular signaling, providing a biological framework for how these sensitivities develop and function.

Sensitive to Frequency, Not to Fault

Autistic children are often highly sensitive to sound, texture, light, and vibration. From a metaphysical standpoint, this makes sense: they are frequency-sensitive beings. Many parents report their children reacting to the hum of electronics, the flicker of fluorescent lighting, or the static between people's emotions.

Because they are tuned in to energetic wavelengths, they may communicate in ways that do not involve words. Some use gesture, sound, art, or movement. Others express themselves through musical instruments, numbers, or pattern creation. These are not *"quirks."* They are languages of vibration. Neuroscientist Candace Pert discovered the "molecules of emotion," showing that feelings move through the body as chemical messengers. Autistic children often seem especially attuned to these signals, registering emotional shifts almost instantly.

Their silence does not mean absence. It means presence, just on a channel we may not be used to tuning into.

Morphic Fields and Group Memory

Rupert Sheldrake's concept of morphic resonance suggests that memory and behavior patterns are not just stored in the brain but shared across members of a species through invisible energetic fields. This means that some children may come into the world already "tuned in" to ancestral or collective frequencies.

Autistic children often seem to access information they have never been taught. They may demonstrate advanced knowledge of certain topics, solve puzzles intuitively, or understand emotional undercurrents without ever being told.

Perhaps they are remembering what we have forgotten. Could they be accessing a form of group memory through their heightened sensitivity?

The Cleve Backster Effect

Backster's experiments showed that plants react to human thought and intention, even from a distance. This response pattern was not based on touch or speech, but on energy. Autistic children often show similar patterns: reacting to intention before action, withdrawing when energies feel off, or moving toward someone with a kind thought.

One teacher observed that her autistic student would physically recoil before a disruptive noise happened, almost as if he sensed the shift in energy before the event. Another child began drawing animals that classmates were silently thinking about.

These are not coincidences but communications, expressed in a language we have lost fluency in.

Star Origins and Dimensional Bridges

Many metaphysical practitioners believe that autistic children may come from or carry memory of higher dimensions or star origins. They may carry codes of advanced consciousness, crystalline DNA structures, or soul contracts tied to planetary evolution.

Unpacking the New Ideas

Crystalline DNA: A metaphysical concept referring to DNA that vibrates at higher frequencies, potentially enabling expanded consciousness, multidimensional perception, and spiritual communication.

Dimensional Bridges: Beings or individuals who can connect and navigate across multiple dimensions of consciousness, serving as translators between worlds.

Star Origins: The idea that some souls incarnate on Earth from other planetary systems to assist in humanity's evolution.

These children may not "*fit*" easily into the third-dimensional matrix because their consciousness is not bound by it. The dense emotions, noise, toxins, and ego-based constructs of this realm may feel abrasive or nonsensical to them. In truth, they are not broken; they are emissaries of a new paradigm.

Seen through this lens, autism is not a disorder but a difference, a sacred divergence meant to anchor higher light into a world that often forgets its divine origins.

This would explain why many autistic children are naturally drawn to symbols, geometric patterns, or certain tones. They may be remembering frequencies from other star systems or holding templates of truth that have yet to be decoded by society.

One parent recalled her daughter humming a sequence of tones nightly, tones that, when analyzed, matched ancient *solfeggio frequencies* associated with DNA repair and spiritual awakening. Another child insisted on drawing a specific spiral every day, later recognized as a sacred-geometry glyph tied to Lemurian teachings.

We must ask: Who are we to dismiss these transmissions? And what do we miss when we do?

Bridging the Gap

When we stop trying to make autistic children *normal* and begin listening, truly listening, to the way they communicate, we open the door to an entirely different form of interaction.

Some parents report developing a silent bond with their child. They begin sensing what their child wants before they ask. They begin receiving images, feelings, and inner nudges. This is telepathy. This marks the return of a forgotten language.

Honoring the Silent Wisdom

Autistic children may be among the *clearest telepathic communicators* alive today. But they speak in vibrations, not just in words. They ask us to slow down. To listen with our hearts. To question what "normal" really means.

They are not lost in silence; they are inviting us in.

In honoring their language, we remember our own.

And in doing so, we may just remember who we truly are.

Science Note

Dr. Candace Pert, who discovered the *molecules of emotion,* revealed that emotions are not just feelings but biochemical signals that circulate through the body, shaping perception and behavior.

Rosalind Franklin's groundbreaking X-ray diffraction images of DNA laid the foundation for understanding how the body stores and transmits information at a molecular level. Temple Grandin's accounts of her own experience show that heightened sensory perception in autism is not dysfunction, but a different form of knowing.

Dr. Stephen Porges' *Polyvegal Theory* adds that what appears to be social with drawl can actually be a nervous system response to overstimulation.

Dr. Bruce Lipton's work in epigenetics demonstrates how environment and frequency influence cellular signaling, supporting the idea that these sensitivities are biologically grounded.

Biologist Rupert Sheldrake's theory of morphic resonance proposes that memory and behavior can be shared across species through invisible energetic fields.

Cleve Backster's experiments with plants and animals further suggested that consciousness responds to intention and emotion, even across distance.

Together, their research supports the idea that nonverbal children, especially those with autism, are deeply attuned to emotional and energetic communication, even if they do not express it in words.

Practitioner Prompt

Encourage therapists and caregivers to observe nonverbal cues as meaningful communication. Create a 7-day log of:

1. Repetitive gestures or symbols
2. Unspoken energetic reactions
3. Unusual synchronicities or telepathic impressions

At the end of the week, reflect:
- What new patterns did you witness?
- How might these moments shift your approach to connection?

To support this, parents and caregivers can:
- Practice stillness and presence daily

Use visual imagery and emotional clarity when communicating

Ask questions silently and wait for felt impressions

Validate intuitive moments and energetic synchronicities

Protect sensory environments by limiting chaotic spaces, artificial lighting, and overwhelming noise

Surround the child with healing tones, nature sounds, and grounding activities like water play or drumming.

Telepathy Toolbox

These practices help children express their inner worlds without words and invite families to experience connection through sound, symbols, and sensation. Keep them playful and light, letting the child lead wherever possible.

Vibration Drawing

Use art to capture the feeling of a space.

How to do it:

1. Sit with your child in a quiet room.
2. Instead of drawing the objects in the room, invite them to draw how the room feels.
3. Use colors, lines, or shapes to represent energy or mood.
4. Share drawings and compare impressions.

Why it works:

Children often sense environments as vibrations rather than appearances. This exercise validates their intuitive reading of spaces.

Silent Matching Game

Strengthen intuition by "tuning in" to each other's symbols.

How to do it:

1. Parent and child each silently think of a symbol, color, or shape.
2. Without speaking, draw it on separate papers.
3. Reveal and compare drawings.
4. Repeat and notice when patterns begin to overlap.

Why it works:

This practice highlights how often thoughts and images overlap without words, building confidence in shared intuitive awareness.

Tone Together

Explore how sound resonates in the body.

How to do it:

1. Sit facing each other in a relaxed posture.
2. Each person hums a tone that "feels right" in the moment.
3. Gradually combine tones and notice how the vibrations shift in the body.
4. Reflect afterward on what each tone felt like.

Why it works:

Children learn that sound carries energy. Combining tones shows them how resonance creates harmony and connection.

Symbol Show-and-Tell

Practice silent storytelling through symbols.

How to do it:

1. Create a set of simple glyph cards—spirals, stars, waves, or other shapes.
2. Invite your child to pick one.
3. Instead of explaining with words, they use gesture, sound, or expression to show what it means.
4. Switch roles and repeat.

Why it works:

Symbols bypass logic and give children a safe way to share intuitive meaning. Parents learn to "read" communication that goes beyond speech.

Star Blanket Time

Create a ritual of quiet connection wrapped in comfort.

How to do it:

1. Wrap up together in a soft blanket.
2. Play gentle, star-like tones (crystal bowls, chimes, or soft recordings).
3. Sit in silence and invite each person to share impressions afterward—through drawing, gesture, or a single word.

Why it works:

This practice blends physical comfort with energetic attunement. Children often feel safe to share subtle impressions when the environment feels cozy and supportive.

Toolbox Wrap-Up

These activities remind children that energy, sound, and symbols are valid languages of connection. When families hum together, draw feelings, or share silent impressions, they rebuild trust in communication that goes beyond words.

The more playful these practices are, the more children will keep their intuitive channels open. Over time, what begins as a simple game with tones, colors, or symbols becomes a deeper family language of trust. These are not just exercises. They are doorways back to the innate ways of knowing that children carry so naturally.

Invitation

What if silence was not absence, but presence in a pure form?

What if the ones we label "nonverbal" are actually speaking a language older than words?

Your child may not speak the way you do, but they are always communicating, through color, tone, gesture, stillness.

The question is not *"Can they hear me?"*

It is *"Am I willing to hear them differently?"*

Trust the channel between your hearts, and let it guide you back to the sacred language of energy.

Transmission from the Telepathic Ones

You who cannot speak in our language—

We hear you anyway.

You who walk among us, quiet and luminous—

You carry the codes of stars.

We did not come here to be understood by the world—

We came here to remind it how to feel.

When you meet us with your heart—

We will always respond.

Because we were never separate.

Just speaking from the silence.

Up Next

To understand these children fully, we must first understand the silence they come wrapped in.

As we journey into Part Two and start with Chapter 7, we will move beyond childhood and explore how adults, as parents, teachers, and caregivers can reopen their own telepathic channels and reconnect to a deeper way of knowing what was never lost, but once forgotten.

PART TWO:

THE PARENT

The parent must learn again what the child
never forgot.

— Unknown

CHAPTER 7

Rebuilding Telepathic Trust with Your Child

For parents and caregivers seeking to reconnect with their child's innate telepathic ability, the journey begins not with words, but with presence. The exercises in this chapter are designed to rebuild the bridge of silent communication. Children are often waiting for us to remember how to use telepathy.

These practices are not just for parents. Grandparents, siblings, stepparents, and caregivers can use them too; anyone who loves and listens. The silent language of telepathy transcends titles. It responds to connection, not role. The following ideas can be woven into everyday life: meals, walks, bedtime, errands. They help normalize telepathy as part of your family's way of being.

Children naturally live in a world of play, symbols, and sensations. Games are not just entertainment; they are doorways into energetic connection. When we play, we bypass the pressure of performance and enter the heart's quiet frequency. The following practices are designed to reawaken that playful trust.

Story Example

One mother shared how she and her five-year-old son played *Emotion Echo* at bedtime. She silently held a feeling of pride, while gazing into his eyes. Without hesitation, he whispered, "You are proud of me." The mother had tears in her eyes. She had not said a word, but he had felt it, clearly. In that moment, their bond deepened. He began offering silent feelings back in their nightly routine, and their emotional communication became even more fluent without needing language.

Developmental science confirms why play is central to rebuilding trust. Psychiatrist Stuart Brown, M.D. showed that play is a biological necessity, shaping resilience and bonding. Psychologist Lev Vygotsky observed that play creates a *"zone of proximal development,"* where children stretch beyond their current abilities through imagination. And Jean Piaget called play the work of childhood, the way children construct knowledge through direct experience. These insights explain why the practices in this chapter emphasize play as the gateway to telepathic connection.

Science Note

Research from the HeartMath Institute shows that when two people intentionally generate heart-based emotions like gratitude or love, their heart rhythms can synchronize, even at a distance. Psychiatrist Daniel Siegel's h on interpersonal neurobiology suggest that this kind of resonance helps rebuild trust between caregivers and children. Developmental researchers agree that play is the natural gateway for this kind of connection: Stuart Brown, M.D. demonstrated that play is essential for trust and resilience, Lev Vygotsky showed that imaginative play creates a bridge into higher learning, and Jean Piaget called play the work of childhood itself. Together, these perspectives affirm that play is not optional; it is the very ground where telepathic trust is rebuilt.

Practitioner Prompt

Create a daily, three-minute ritual of silent mirroring with your child.
- No words, no correction; just presence.
- Write down what each of you felt afterward.

Over time, note if your child's openness and calmness increase. This simple act rewires trust and creates a shared field of knowing.

Telepathy Toolbox

This chapter may seem different from the previous chapters. That is because telepathy is not an idea to only be understood; it is a practice to be lived. The tools you will find here are not side notes; they are the text itself. They teach how the parent and child rebuild trust, moment by moment, and help parents restore the silent language they once knew.

These practices may seem too simple, but they are profound. They reawaken dormant pathways of connection and honor the language before words. Telepathy is not magic; it is a normal function that our children are waiting for us to remember and reclaim together.

Image Sharing Game

This simple practice teaches children how to send and receive images silently, building confidence in their telepathic awareness.

How to do it:

1. Sit across from your child in a quiet space.
2. Think of a simple image (like a sun, cat, or flower).
3. Ask your child to describe or draw what they sense.
4. Switch roles after a few minutes.

Why it works:

Starting with playful categories your child loves keeps the practice light. Success is measured not in perfect accuracy but in shared joy and connection.

Story Snapshots

This activity invites your child to practice receiving more complex images, strengthening their ability to tune into visual telepathy.

How to do it:

1. Think of a short scene—for example, a park with a dog chasing a ball—and visualize it vividly in your mind.
2. Invite your child to describe the image or draw what they sense.
3. Switch roles. Your child creates the scene; you receive it.

Why it works:

Scenes add layers of detail—movement, setting, and characters—which help children expand their telepathic "bandwidth." The playful exchange also builds confidence and turns telepathy into a shared creative game.

Picture Ping-Pong

This practice creates a playful back-and-forth, turning telepathy into a visual "conversation" between you and your child.

How to do it:

1. Parent sends an image mentally.
2. Child receives and then sends back a new image.
3. Parent receives and continues the "visual conversation."

Why it works:

The game builds a sense of dialogue without words, helping children trust that telepathy can flow both ways. It also encourages creativity and strengthens connection through shared imagination.

Heart Coherence Breathing

This calming exercise aligns parent and child energetically, opening the heart channel for deeper telepathic connection.

How to do it:

1. Sit together and place a hand over your hearts.
2. Breathe in slowly to a count of four, hold for two, and exhale for six.
3. As you breathe, visualize love or gratitude.
4. Continue for three to five minutes.

Why it works:

Telepathy flows best when energy fields are coherent. This practice brings your heart and your child's heart into resonance, creating a physiological foundation for trust and silent communication.

Heartbeat Match

This practice deepens awareness of subtle rhythms and strengthens the energetic bond between parent and child.

How to do it:

1. Each person closes their eyes and tunes into the rhythm of the other's heartbeat. You may place a hand gently over the other's heart, or simply imagine it.
2. Try to match your breathing or movement to that rhythm.

Why it works:

Synchronizing with another person's heartbeat creates a powerful sense of unity. This exercise fosters calm, trust, and beautiful resonance.

As you move through these practices, remember: it is not about accuracy or perfection. It is about creating a field of safety where your child's silent knowing can reemerge without fear of being judged. Playfulness is the key.

Heart Whisper

This activity invites silent emotional exchange, helping children recognize feelings without words.

How to do it:

1. Begin with coherence breathing to center yourselves.
2. Each person silently "whispers" a feeling through their heart to the other.
3. Open your eyes and guess what the other person sent.

Why it works:

By practicing heart-to-heart communication, children strengthen emotional intuition. This playful guessing game validates that feelings can be shared without words.

Mutual Silence and Mirroring

This practice helps parent and child settle into stillness together, allowing subtle energetic communication to emerge naturally.

How to do it:

1. Sit or lie down facing your child, with no toys, screens, or distractions.
2. Make gentle eye contact or simply allow a natural gaze.
3. Mirror your child's expressions or movements without speaking.
4. Let thoughts fade and simply *be* with one another.

Why it works:

Shared silence builds an energetic bond that words cannot reach. By mirroring each other gently, you create a field of safety and presence where spontaneous knowing often arises.

Mirror Me Play

This playful exercise strengthens empathy and intuition by blending movement, expression, and emotion.

How to do it:

1. Set a timer for one minute.
2. One person leads subtle movements, facial expressions, or gestures.

3. The other mirrors them precisely.

4. Switch roles and reflect after each turn on how you felt.

5. Add an *Emotion Echo*: one person silently feels an emotion and shows it on their face while the other guesses and mirrors it.

Why it works:

Mirroring fosters deep attunement. Adding the Emotion Echo encourages sensitivity to energy and emotional nuance, teaching children to read and reflect feelings without words.

Thought Transmission Practice

This activity trains children to recognize mental imagery and strengthens their confidence in telepathic perception.

How to do it:

1. Choose a set of objects (such as three toys or cards).

2. The parent silently selects one, visualizing it strongly.

3. The child tries to sense which object was chosen.

4. Switch roles so the child gets to "send" as well.

Why it works:

By working with simple, familiar objects, children learn to trust the impressions they receive. Families often find surprising accuracy emerges when sessions are short, playful, and pressure-free.

Guess the Number

This quick and simple game helps children practice tuning into mental focus and intention.

How to do it:

1. Parent silently chooses a number between 1 and 5.

2. Child relaxes, tunes in, and guesses.

3. As skill develops, gradually increase the number range.

Why it works:

Numbers are clear and simple targets for telepathic practice. Expanding the range slowly builds confidence while keeping the game fun and approachable.

Telepathic Charades

This lively game blends imagination, action, and silent communication.

How to do it:

1. Parent thinks of an action (like brushing teeth or jumping rope) and holds it in mind.

2. Send the action silently.

3. Child guesses and performs the action.

4. Switch roles for even more fun.

Why it works:

Actions are easier to sense than abstract thoughts, making this game highly engaging. It brings laughter and movement into telepathy practice, helping children stay relaxed and playful while developing their intuitive skills.

Emotion Radar

This game helps children practice sensing emotions around them without relying on words.

How to do it:

1. Ask your child to close their eyes and "scan" the room.

2. Have them describe how others are feeling, even if only one other person is present.

3. Encourage them to share the "*feeling image*" or color they sense.

Why it works:

Children often perceive emotions as colors, images, or sensations. By validating their impressions, you strengthen their trust in their intuitive senses.

Deck of Intuition

This activity uses a deck of simple playing cards to help children practice receiving impressions and symbols.

How to do it:

1. One family member selects a card to send telepathically.
2. The others close their eyes and "tune in" to the sender.
3. Share impressions: What image comes to mind? What color? What number?
4. Celebrate closeness as well as correctness.

Why it works:

The focus is on practicing intuitive sensing rather than getting the "right" answer. This builds confidence and reinforces that telepathy is about connection, not perfection.

One Minute of Shared Stillness

This exercise cultivates presence and helps families reconnect without distraction.

How to do it:

1. Sit together and agree to one minute of total silence.
2. During that minute, simply notice your breath and inner feelings.
3. Afterward, share what you "heard" or sensed inside.

Why it works:

Even one minute of silence can reset energy and open telepathic channels. Done daily, it becomes a ritual of presence and shared awareness.

Tuning Into the Emotional Field

This practice teaches parents to listen beyond words, responding to what their child feels rather than only what they say.

How to do it:

1. When your child is upset, pause before reacting.
2. Breathe deeply and inwardly ask: *"What does my child need right now?"*
3. Notice any sudden feelings, images, or words that arise.
4. Offer support based on those impressions.

Why it works:

Children communicate as much through energy as they do through words. By pausing and attuning, you often discover the right response without your child needing to explain.

Sound Ping

This playful practice uses tones and rhythms to create a shared "sound story," helping children link vibration with feeling and imagery.

How to do it:

1. Sit together in a circle.
2. One person makes a tone (such as a hum, whistle, or tap).
3. The next person repeats it and adds their own tone.
4. Continue around the circle for three to four rounds.
5. Pause and ask: *"What feeling or image did that sound story tell?"*

Why it works:

Sound carries vibration that children naturally respond to. This exercise shows them how energy can be expressed and interpreted without words, strengthening intuitive listening and imagination.

Feel and Draw

This activity helps children express emotions through color and imagery, strengthening the link between feelings and intuition.

How to do it:

1. Parent and child quietly tune into a shared emotion (such as joy, calm, or excitement).
2. Without speaking, each draws or colors what that emotion feels like.
3. Share the drawings and discuss impressions afterward.

Why it works:

Children often communicate feelings more easily through art than words. This practice validates their inner world and shows that emotions can be "seen" and shared silently.

Journaling and Dream Sharing

Recording dreams and impressions teaches children that their inner world has value and strengthens telepathic memory.

How to do it:

1. Keep a dream journal by both your bed and your child's.
2. Each morning, write or draw anything remembered from dreams.
3. Share what you recorded with one another.

Why it works:

Dreams often carry symbolic telepathic messages. Many parents find they dream the same symbols or feelings as their children, or even appear in each other's dreams. Journaling makes these hidden connections visible.

Telepathy Journal

A shared journal helps families notice patterns of silent communication in everyday life.

How to do it:

1. Keep a special notebook labeled *Telepathy Journal*.

2. Record moments when you "just knew" what your child was thinking, or when your child voiced something you were silently holding.
3. Review the entries together each week.

Why it works:

Patterns of connection become clearer over time. Recording and reflecting affirms the silent bond you already share.

Drawing the Dream

Turning dream symbols into pictures helps children see and trust their inner language.

How to do it:

1. After waking, both parent and child draw one image from their dream.
2. Compare the symbols or emotions to see overlap.
3. Keep drawings abstract or literal—it is about expression, not accuracy.

Why it works:

Dreams often reveal shared feelings or parallel symbols. This activity makes the invisible visible, deepening trust in intuitive communication.

Dream Pick-Up

This game shows how thoughts before sleep can influence the dream world.

How to do it:

1. Before bedtime, one person begins a short dream story (e.g., *"Tonight, we will fly over a glowing forest"*).
2. The other person continues the story the next morning, sharing what they dreamed.
3. Compare to see how closely the dreams aligned.

Why it works:

By planting seeds in the dream state, families discover how thoughts carry over into the night. It highlights the subtle ways minds stay connected even in sleep.

Building Two-Way Trust

At the heart of telepathy is trust, not guessing. Children will only share openly if they feel safe and believed. This practice helps parents model encouragement and openness so the channel stays strong.

How to do it:

1. Honor even the smallest attempt by responding warmly. Say things like, *"I love that you picked up on that,"* or *"Yes, I was just thinking about that!"*

2. Invite your child to take the lead. Ask, *"What am I thinking right now?"* or, *"Can you send me a message?"*

3. Celebrate every effort, whether or not the message was "accurate."

Why it works:

When children feel validated, their confidence in silent communication grows. Laughter, play, and lightness keep telepathy from feeling like a test. The more relaxed the atmosphere, the more open the channel becomes.

Everyday Applications

Telepathy does not have to be a special event—it can become part of daily life. These practices weave silent connection into ordinary moments.

How to do it:

1. When you are apart, silently send your child loving thoughts— for example, while they are at school—and later ask if they "felt" it.

2. In busy places like a store, instead of calling your child aloud, think *"come here"* silently and observe their response.

3. At bedtime, send calming thoughts before speaking; many children respond more deeply to the energy than the words.

Why it works:

Small daily practices normalize telepathy as part of family life. Children learn that silent communication is real, reliable, and woven into everyday experiences.

Play-Based Expansion Ideas

Games keep telepathy lighthearted, helping children stay relaxed while building confidence.

How to do it:

- **Color Sending**: Use a deck of colorful cards. Focus on one color and have your child guess which it is. Increase difficulty as their skill grows.

- **Telepathic Hide-and-Seek**: One person hides an object; the other tries to sense its location. This blends fun with intuitive practice.

- **Mood Matching**: Without speaking, each person tries to feel into the other's mood, then draw or write it down. Share and compare afterward.

- **Soundless Storytelling**: Parent silently thinks of a short story and conveys it through images and emotions. The child then draws or retells what they received.

Why it works:

Play allows children to stretch their abilities without pressure. These games nurture both intuition and trust, making telepathy a shared adventure rather than a test.

Tips for Strengthening the Parent's Skills

Telepathy is a two-way channel. The more attuned and relaxed you are, the more easily your child will connect with you. These simple practices help parents strengthen their side of the bridge.

How to do it:

1. **Practice daily meditation** to quiet the analytical mind and open the intuitive one. Even five minutes of stillness makes a difference.

2. **Tune into your child's presence** when you are apart. Silently ask, *"What might they be feeling right now?"* and notice what impressions arise.

3. **Spend time in nature together**. Natural environments calm the nervous system, making intuitive and telepathic communication easier to access.

Why it works:

Children sense when parents are scattered or preoccupied. By cultivating presence, calm, and curiosity, you model the very qualities that make telepathy flow.

When the Channel Feels Blocked

Even with practice, there will be times when telepathic connection feels fuzzy or distant. This is normal and often points to simple, practical causes.

How to do it:

1. **Check for EMF exposure.** Too much screen time or proximity to strong Wi-Fi can dull sensitivity.

2. **Clear emotional residue.** If there is tension, anger, or sadness, acknowledge it gently before returning to intuitive play.

3. **Address physical needs.** Hunger, fatigue, or overstimulation can override openness.

Why it works:

Resetting the environment—through a breath, a smile, or a lighthearted return to an exercise—helps reopen the channel. Telepathy thrives in calm, balanced states.

Making It a Lifestyle

Telepathy does not need to be scheduled like homework. It can become a natural part of everyday life.

How to do it:

1. Use it in simple moments: while cooking, walking, or driving. Silently send your child a thought or feeling.

2. Let your child know you were thinking of them through a smile, a gesture, or a quiet acknowledgment.

3. Reinforce intuitive hits by saying, "I had a feeling you would say that!"

Why it works:

Normalizing telepathy in daily life makes it feel natural rather than forced. Small gestures of recognition weave intuition into the fabric of family connection.

Creating Rituals of Connection

Building small rituals keeps the bond alive and sacred, giving children regular opportunities to practice their intuitive gifts.

How to do it:

1. **Telepathic Check-ins**: Before bedtime, close your eyes together and silently ask: *"How was your day?"* Exchange feelings or images.

2. **Energy Hugs**: Even when apart, imagine wrapping your child in a loving energy hug and invite them to send one back.

3. **Synchronicity Noticing**: Keep track of times when you and your child think or say the same thing. Reflect on what these moments reveal.

Why it works:

Rituals anchor the invisible into the visible. They create a dependable rhythm where trust, synchronicity, and silent communication can flourish.

Toolbox Wrap-Up

When you look back on these games, you will notice a pattern: each one is a way of saying, "I trust you. I hear you. I believe in you."

Telepathy is not rebuilt through lectures or logic; it is rebuilt through shared experiences that bypass the mind and speak directly to the heart. Whether you are humming together, exchanging images, keeping a telepathy journal, or sending a message at bedtime, each activity is planting seeds of presence and trust.

Some days the connection will feel strong; other days it may seem faint. Both are part of the process. The goal is not accuracy or perfection—it is remembering the language that was always there.

As you make these practices part of daily life, you will find telepathy becoming less like an exercise and more like a natural rhythm of family life. It is not about creating something new; it is about uncovering what was never lost. In every smile, every image, every quiet pause, you are remembering together.

Invitation

Rebuilding trust does not mean reciting the perfect words. It means showing up, heart open and still.

Every quiet breath, every shared glance, every silly game sends a message: I trust you. I hear you. I remember.

You do not need to push for connection. Just return to presence.

That is where telepathy lives.

That is where you will find each other.

Transmission from the Telepathic Ones

We speak not with mouths, but with moments.

You feel us more than hear us.

When you slow down, we become louder.

When you listen, we are clearer.

You do not have to become us.

Only remember you once were.

Up Next:

You are now ready to explore the deeper layers behind this connection. In Chapter 8, we will explore the spiritual and scientific overlap that explains why these telepathic pathways exist and how to support their reawakening in yourself and your community.

CHAPTER 8

The Language Before Words

Before words, there was *Light*.

Before syllables were shaped by tongue or teeth, there were pulses of knowing, waves of emotion, images bright as memory and true as breath. This chapter explores that primal language, the vibrational tongue of the soul, and how we can remember it again.

What Is Vibrational Language?

Vibrational language is the communication system of the soul. It is not constrained by alphabet or dialect.

It speaks in:

- Light: bursts of inner vision, flashes of color or form
- Sound: tones, harmonics, ringing or music in the mind
- Emotion: waves of feeling that carry deep information
- Color and Image: symbolic impressions that bypass logic

When Babies See the Field

You have likely experienced this. The way a baby responds to a soothing hum. The pull you feel when someone silently enters a room. A *gut feeling* so strong it turns your head before a word is spoken. These are not coincidences; they are communications.

Watch a baby in a restaurant, an airport, or even in your own living room. Long before they can speak, they see. Their gaze will suddenly shift to something across the room, their eyes fixed on an invisible dance of color or movement you cannot perceive. You might dangle a shiny mobile above their crib—glimmering lights, soothing music—and yet their attention drifts elsewhere, to a corner of the room where nothing "should" be. But the child knows better. They are watching energy, not objects. They are tracking light, not distraction. They are responding to a multidimensional field that our adult eyes have forgotten how to notice. Here is an example of a channeled perspective confirming this phenomenon:

> *This example is deeply aligned the Lee Carroll's recently channeled guidance from KRYON about children's telepathic abilities and how much society has to gain from helping children stay this way and helping parents reawaken their own telepathic nature.*

> *Telepathy sustains the love in families and a key foundation of society. KRYON's message could not have been timed more perfectly. (See APPENDIX G: Children Still See the Other Side.)*

Author Lynne McTaggart's research in *The Field* echoes this truth: intention and emotion can move invisibly between people, shaping outcomes even across distance. What we feel is already a form of communication.

The Soul's Way of Speaking Before Incarnation

Before birth, communication is vibrational. In utero, a baby does not "hear" language in the way we think, they feel it. Emotions, tone, intent. They read energy fields long before they understand sentences.

Many spiritual traditions agree: before we incarnate, we exist in a state of unity, communicating through pure intention and resonance. We "speak" through shared light patterns, emotional fields, and harmonic resonance.

This pre-birth memory often lingers in very young children, explaining why many toddlers seem to know things they were never taught, such as when they say *"before I came here"* or '*the place I was before.*" It also explains why some children resist spoken language, because it feels like a downgrade or lesser form of communication from something much richer and clearer.

Restoring the *Language of Light* begins by reattuning to this soul-level memory.

Scientist Rosalind Franklin's pioneering X-ray diffraction images revealed the elegant structure of DNA, showing that pattern, vibration, and light are literally encoded in our cells. This reminds us that the "language of light" children often remember is not just spiritual poetry, but a biological truth written into the body itself.

Activating Your Intuitive Channels as an Adult

The first step to reclaiming this lost fluency is to quiet the mind and awaken the senses beyond the physical.

Science Note

Lynne McTaggart's research in *The Field* demonstrates that human intention can influence people, objects, and even future events across space and time. Her findings validate what intuitive families already sense: images, emotions, and knowing can move invisibly between us.

Rosalind Franklin's pioneering X-ray diffraction images of DNA revealed its elegant structure as a carrier of information, reminding us that our very biology is designed for storage, transmission, and reception. Her work with DNA reminds us that pattern, vibration, and light are not abstract metaphors. Instead, they are biological realities encoded in our cells.

The wide range of research noted in this book affirms that the *light language* our children speak is both poetic and profoundly real.

Vibrational Awareness Log

This practice helps caregivers, teachers, or therapists notice and validate the subtle nonverbal ways children communicate.

How to do it:

1. Keep a shared log for seven days with a child or client.
2. Each day, write down one nonverbal impression you received; it might be an emotion, image, tone, or color.
3. Reflect together: *How did that impression affect our connection?*
4. Encourage symbolic sharing (drawing, colors, gestures) when words feel too small.

Why it works:

You will be surprised how often vibrational sharing is more accurate than words. Children often communicate deep emotion without speaking at all. Meeting them at the level of frequency, instead of only behavior, transforms both connection and trust.

It is we adults who must learn to listen again. The task belongs to us. Can we remember how to listen?

Telepathy Toolbox

These practices help reactivate your innate ability to communicate through vibration, feeling, image, and sound. They are not magic tricks; they are memory. Each one is a doorway back to connection. Try them lightly, with curiosity, and see how your family's intuitive language begins to reawaken.

The Inner Eye (Clairvoyance)

This practice awakens your natural ability to "see" with inner vision.

How to do it:

1. Sit quietly in meditation and visualize light or images.

2. Ask yourself: "What image matches how I feel right now?"

3. Let symbolic visions rise without analyzing—just notice.

Why it works:

Children often think in images before words. Practicing visualization strengthens the same intuitive channel they naturally use.

The Inner Ear (Clairaudience)

Tune into subtle sounds and messages beyond ordinary hearing.

How to do it:

1. Sit in silence and ask inwardly for one word or tone your child (or higher self) wants you to hear today.

2. Pay attention to what comes—a hum, whisper, rhythm, or even a song fragment.

3. Record what you notice, even if it feels small.

Why it works:

Noticing subtle tones validates that telepathic impressions can arrive as vibration, not just thought.

The Inner Heart (Clairsentience)

Strengthen emotional intuition—the ability to feel what is unsaid.

How to do it:

1. Focus on your chest center.

2. Feel into the emotional tone of a space, person, or thought.

3. Ask: "What does this emotion want me to know?" and listen with your heart.

Why it works:

Children communicate more through feelings than logic. This practice helps adults attune to that same natural language.

The Knowing Core (Claircognizance)

Build trust in the sudden flashes of inner knowing.

How to do it:

1. Each time you "just know," pause and record it in a journal.
2. Look back for patterns or validations.
3. Share your experiences with your child so they see knowing is natural.

Why it works:

Validating intuitive knowing makes it stronger. It shows children their unexplainable insights are trustworthy.

Light Mapping

Receive visual impressions from your child's soul energy.

How to do it:

1. Sit in a dim, quiet space with eyes closed.
2. Ask inwardly: "What light is my child's soul showing me?"
3. Notice shapes, colors, or pulses behind your eyelids.
4. Draw what you saw afterward.

Why it works:

Light impressions connect you to your child's soul-level communication. Drawing them makes the invisible visible.

Tone Matching

A playful sound game for family resonance.

How to do it:

1. Sit quietly and begin humming softly.
2. Let the pitch change naturally.

3. After one to two minutes, invite your child to hum a sound that "feels right."
4. Compare and notice if tones match or harmonize.

Why it works:

Sound is vibration, and vibration is telepathy's foundation. Matching tones creates shared frequency awareness.

Emotion Weaving

Turn emotions into energetic threads.

How to do it:

1. Choose a strong feeling (love, joy, peace).
2. Imagine weaving it into a glowing cord of light.
3. Send the "cord" from your heart to your child's.
4. Ask silently if they felt it.

Why it works:

Children sense emotions as energy. Weaving them into light strengthens trust and makes invisible love tangible.

Color Codes

A playful way to express feelings through color.

How to do it:

1. Together, assign colors to feelings (e.g., red = strong, blue = calm).
2. Create a chart or simple deck of cards.
3. Use them daily for mood check-ins.

Why it works:

Symbolic color language builds emotional literacy. Children learn to describe subtle states without needing words.

Light Language Cards

Develop a family-specific symbolic language.

How to do it:

1. Cut blank cards and draw symbols, spirals, or shapes that feel meaningful.
2. Invite your child to create their own.
3. Use them to communicate simple needs or feelings silently.

Why it works:

Over time, your family develops a unique symbolic language, strengthening trust and nonverbal connection.

Breath and Beam

Blend breathwork and visualization to strengthen the heart-to-heart bond.

How to do it:

1. Sit back-to-back and breathe together in rhythm.
2. Imagine a beam of light connecting your hearts.
3. Silently send gratitude or love down the beam.
4. When ready, turn around and share how it felt.

Why it works:

Breathing synchronizes the nervous system, and the visualization amplifies intention. Together, they create a tangible sense of unseen connection.

Light Bath Meditation

Use light as a healing and communicative force.

How to do it:

1. Lie down in a quiet, darkened room.

2. Imagine golden-white light pouring over you and your child.

3. Breathe together as you "soak" in the light.

4. Share afterward what images or messages arose.

Why it works:

Light imagery relaxes the body and strengthens inner vision, creating a sacred space where intuitive impressions surface naturally.

Sound Sculpting

Create emotional storytelling through tones.

How to do it:

1. Gather objects that make different sounds (bells, bowls, shakers).

2. Play one sound and ask your child what feeling it matches.

3. Invite them to create a "sound story" using tones.

Why it works:

Sound carries vibration and meaning. Sound stories teach children how emotions can be expressed musically and symbolically.

Aura Portraits

The aim is to express and interpret energetic fields through art.

Auras are like a transparent haze around the head and shoulders. In this exercise, you "view" your own aura.

The more common practice has the subject sitting in front of a plain, white background while the other gazes to see the haze.

In both cases, perception can improve through practice.

How to do it:

1. Ask your child to close their eyes and imagine their aura color.

2. Do the same for yourself.

3. Each of you draws what you saw, e.g., a stick figure or bubble person.

4. Use crayons, chalk, or colored pencils to add the colors.

Share and discuss what each color means. Additional reference guides are widely available online.

Why it works:

Aura portraits validate that subtle impressions are real and worth sharing. They open conversations about energy and emotion. Your child may already see auras and start asking questions.

Mirror Spark

Deepen nonverbal resonance through presence.

How to do it:

1. Sit face-to-face and gaze softly into each other's eyes.
2. Allow laughter, tears, or stillness to arise naturally.
3. After two to three minutes, describe what light or feeling you saw reflected.

Why it works:

Eye contact without words creates profound attunement. Presence itself becomes a language.

Dream Language Journal

Use dreams as channels of symbolic communication.

How to do it:

1. Keep a shared dream journal.
2. Each morning, draw or write dream symbols, colors, or feelings.
3. Look together for recurring images or themes.

Why it works:

Dreams reveal subconscious and telepathic connections. Recording them validates that the inner world is just as real as the outer one.

Everyday Integration

Vibrational awareness is not meant to be practiced once in a while—it belongs in the fabric of daily family life. These simple ideas weave telepathy into ordinary moments.

How to do it:

1. Use color in conversation: ask, *"What color was your day?"* and let them answer with a hue instead of words.

2. Replace words with sound: hum, sing, or whisper a tone together.

3. Draw emotions: sit side-by-side and draw how you feel.

4. Light rituals: place a candle at the table and send thoughts through the flame.

5. Morning vibe checks: begin the day by asking, *"What is your vibration today?"*

6. Silent Storytime: imagine the same scene quietly, then draw it and compare.

7. Sound resets: clear energy with bells, chimes, or bowls before bedtime.

8. Shared visuals: say, *"Let us dream in rainbow light tonight,"* and hold the image together.

9. Symbols of support: create a "symbol of the week" to silently send when someone needs love.

10. Vibe journals: record daily impressions, colors, or feelings.

11. Crystal messages: whisper a thought into a crystal for your child to carry.

12. Anchored intentions: pair oils or essences with a silent thought.

13. Lunchbox notes without words: silently send a message while packing lunch.

14. Family sound of the week: pick a tone, hum, or bell to use as a reset signal.

Why it works:

Infusing daily routines with color, sound, symbols, and intention normalizes telepathic connection. Children learn intuition is not rare—it is part of everyday life.

Toolbox Wrap-Up

This chapter may look different from the ones before it, because telepathy is not only an idea to understand; it is a practice to live. These tools are not side notes; they are the text itself. They are how parents and children rebuild trust, moment by moment.

Some practices are quiet and reflective, others playful and energetic. Together, they form a language before words: a living reminder that connection flows through light, sound, feeling, and image.

If the list feels long, remember you do not need to do them all. Choose one or two that feel natural, and let them become part of your rhythm. Telepathy grows not through pressure, but through presence. Each small attempt plants a seed of trust. Over time, those seeds grow into the living language you and your child never truly lose.

Invitation

The *Language of Light* is already within you. It does not need to be learned; only remembered. Let it rise in your presence, in your play, in your parenting. Allow the silence between words to become a space of shared understanding. Whether you hum, draw, gaze, or send emotion on a beam of breath, you are practicing telepathy. You are saying: I see you. I feel you. I remember.

Return to this language daily. It will speak back.

Transmission from the Temple of Light

You were born fluent in *Light*.

You sang before you spoke.

You saw truth before it was named.

This is not a new skill.

It is a reawakening.

Let the tones rise again.

Let your inner eye reopen.

Your child is already singing.

Will you remember how to sing it?

Up Next:

As we move forward, we will explore what happens when this language is dismissed, and how that dismissal often leads to suppression, misdiagnosis, and misunderstanding.

CHAPTER 9

Schools of the Future

In classrooms of the future, silence no longer signals boredom or disengagement. It signals communion.

Teachers and students connect not only through words but also through frequency, emotion, and resonance. This is the age of vibrational education where telepathy is nurtured, intuition is honored, and learning flows in more than one language.

These schools do not replace reading and writing; they transcend them. Language remains important, but it is no longer the only, or even the primary, method of communication. In these visionary environments, children learn how to both speak and sense, to calculate and intuit, to analyze and feel.

What if a teacher could feel that a child was overwhelmed without needing to ask? What if a child could transmit a question telepathically while still learning to form it into words? What if tests were not based on memorized facts but on demonstrated resonance with core concepts, expressed in images, light, tone, or gesture?

These practices are not just for parents. Grandparents, siblings, stepparents, and caregivers can use them too, anyone who loves and listens. The future school welcomes all beings of heart, not just those with titles.

Intuition-Based Learning Models

Montessori and Waldorf schools have already paved the way by honoring the child's inner rhythm and developmental timing. But future schools go even further. Here, learning is not imposed. It is revealed. Psychiatrist Dr. Dan Siegel's work in interpersonal neurobiology confirms why: when classrooms nurture shared emotional resonance, memory and learning strengthen, and children feel safe to explore beyond words.

Advanced Studies in Consciousness

Once students have mastered the basics of telepathic connection, they may move into advanced explorations of consciousness—practices that stretch the boundaries of what the mind and energy field can do.

Examples of advanced studies include:

1. **Energy Shaping** – Using intention to bend spoons or reshape matter as an exercise in will and focus.

2. **Telekinesis Experiments** – Moving objects through subtle energy, for example, floating ping-pong balls on waves of sound or air guided by thought.

3. **Mind Over Matter Games** – Altering outcomes by influencing dice rolls, spinning tops, or roulette wheels, learning how focused resonance interacts with probability.

4. **Healing Transmission** – Channeling restorative energy to support plants, animals, or classmates, discovering the impact of directed compassion.

5. **Teleportation Visualization** – Practicing advanced imagery and presence exercises to explore the principles behind remote awareness and nonlocal connection.

Why it works:

These studies are not about spectacle, but about training focus, resonance, and ethical responsibility. They help students recognize that consciousness is not confined to the brain; it is a field that shapes reality.

Ethical Awareness

With power comes responsibility. These schools emphasize ethics as much as skill. Children are taught:

Consent in telepathy: Never 'read' without permission.

Emotional hygiene: Clear your field before engaging in energy exchange.

Energetic boundaries: Keep your aura clean and respectful.

This emphasis ensures that expanded perception does not become manipulation. Instead, it fosters mutual respect and connection.

Teacher as Facilitator, Not Authority

In the schools of the future, teachers are not just instructors; they are facilitators of energy and resonance.

Their roles include:

1. **Frequency guides** – helping students find their vibrational match for ideas and actions.
2. **Energy readers** – sensing the emotional tone of the room and adjusting activities accordingly.
3. **Intuition mentors** – modeling inner listening and spontaneous knowing.
4. **Emotional stabilizers** – guiding regulation and coherence when emotional turbulence arises.

Rather than impose knowledge, these educators co-create it. They read subtle fields to know when to speak or pause. Their very presence becomes a harmonic tuning fork, helping each student find resonance.

Studies from HeartMath Institute show that when groups breathe and focus together, their heart rhythms synchronize, creating coherence in the room. Imagine a classroom where learning begins not with bells, but with resonance.

Future School Curriculum Ideas

Subjects Might Include:

The curriculum of future schools blends science, spirit, and subtle energy into living subjects that awaken the whole child.

1. **Vibrational Geometry** – Exploring how shapes and sacred patterns arise from frequency, teaching students that form is frozen vibration.
2. **Emotional Frequencies** – Learning to read and shift one's own emotional field for healing, clarity, and resilience.
3. **Energy Technology** – Designing and building subtle energy tools such as crystal grids, tensor rings, and light-encoded wands.

113

4. **Quantum Arts** – Practicing manifestation training, conscious time selection, and working with parallel timelines as creative exercises.

5. **Group Coherence** – Engaging in heart-brain synchronization to amplify telepathy, peace, and collective learning.

6. **Earth Wisdom** – Communicating with nature spirits, honoring ley lines, and decoding plant medicine through vibration.

Why it works:

Psychiatrist Dr. Dan Siegel calls this "interpersonal neurobiology"—where shared emotional resonance builds memory, safety, and trust. In these classrooms, the nervous system itself becomes a field of learning, turning education into an embodied, relational experience.

Children Might Choose a Specialty

In the schools of the future, each child is encouraged to deepen their natural gifts by pursuing areas of energetic mastery.

1. **Telepathic Communication** – The art of direct mind-to-mind connection without spoken words. Students cultivate the clarity of their inner voice and practice sending and receiving thoughts, images, emotions, and messages across space and time.

2. **Elemental Alchemy** – Working with the five elements: earth, water, air, fire, and ether, to restore balance and harmony. Students learn to attune with elemental consciousness, gently influence natural forces such as weather, and harmonize environmental energies within and around themselves.

3. **Etheric Architecture** – Designing and creating structures from energy patterns. These may include blueprints for sacred spaces, grid lines, or etheric temples existing in nonphysical dimensions, serving as anchors for healing, meditation, and spiritual growth.

4. **Galactic History** – Exploring humanity's metaphysical records and Earth's relationship to star nations and galactic civilizations. Children uncover their soul origins, planetary migrations, and the unfolding universal timeline from a multidimensional perspective.

5. **Crystal Coding** – Learning the energetic language of crystals. Students practice programming crystals with intentions, frequencies, and healing patterns, charging them with thought, sound, or light. These crystals are then used as tools for memory storage, energy alignment, healing, and communication.

Why it matters:

Schools of the future are not factories of conformity but temples of awakening. They honor the full spectrum of human potential. These learning centers are not fantasy; they are remembering. They reflect what the soul has always known: that we are more than minds, more than bodies, more than test scores or grades.

We are energy, sound, light, and love. And when we teach this way, we create a humanity that does not just survive; it sings.

Science Note

Emerging research validates what intuitive educators and mystics have long sensed: learning is not just cognitive, it is energetic. The HeartMath Institute has shown that the heart's electromagnetic field can synchronize between individuals, especially in classrooms that cultivate coherence.

Psychiatrist Dr. Dan Siegel's work in interpersonal neurobiology confirms that shared emotional resonance enhances memory, behavior, and relational safety. Alternative education pioneers like Montessori and Waldorf demonstrated how honoring a child's rhythm and imagination can transform learning environments. And quantum biologists such as Bruce Lipton suggest that cellular communication is shaped by fields of energy, pointing to the possibility of nonlocal information transfer. In the schools of the future, this science becomes practice.

Reading the Room

If you are an educator or parent, begin each day by sensing the emotional *tone* of the space before anyone speaks. What do you feel in your heart or body? Write it down. Then see if the class confirms or shifts your reading.

Students might practice:

1. **Vibrational Sound Baths** – Listening to knowledge through healing sounds such as crystal singing bowls, Tibetan bowls, or monochords. The vibrations harmonize brainwaves, allowing children to absorb concepts energetically rather than analytically and embed information on a cellular level.

2. **Curriculum Dowsing** – Using pendulums or L-rods to find their most aligned path for the day. By asking, *"What do I most need to learn today?"* the subtle movement of the tool points the way to their next subject or lesson.

3. **Meditative Downloads** – Entering meditative states to access subconscious or superconscious solutions. Instead of memorizing formulas, students intuitively *see* or sense answers, which they then verify after returning to ordinary awareness.

4. **Group Telepathy Sessions** – Practicing silent, focused intention where children transmit ideas, stories, or images telepathically. Recipients draw or describe what they sensed, building not only accuracy but also empathy and trust.

Why it works:

One teacher shared how a child, without speaking, handed them a drawing that mirrored the exact visual meditation the teacher had just held in their mind. The resonance was undeniable. These moments become affirmations that we are all connected in fields of thought and light.

Telepathy Toolbox

These playful, intuitive exercises help children build nonverbal communication, empathy, and energetic awareness. They are perfect for both classroom and homeschool settings.

Mirrored Pairing

This partner exercise strengthens resonance and intuitive sensitivity.

How to do it:

1. Sit silently in pairs.
2. One partner sends a shape, emotion, or image.
3. The other guesses what was sent.
4. Switch roles.

Why it works:

Children learn to tune into subtle impressions from others, building empathy and trust through playful guessing.

Energy Pyramid Building

This activity explores how intention can influence energy fields.

How to do it:

1. Construct small pyramids from straws, wood, or copper wire.
2. "Charge" them together with shared intentions.
3. Observe how plants, crystals, or moods shift when placed inside or near the pyramids.

Why it works:

Pyramids amplify intention and focus. This hands-on activity helps children see how energy can affect both the environment and their own state of being.

Emotion Transmission Game

This playful exercise teaches children how to "send" emotions energetically.

How to do it:

1. One child chooses a feeling and imagines it as a color (e.g., yellow = happy, blue = calm).

2. Without saying it aloud, they silently "send" it to the group.

3. Others draw or name what they received.

4. Compare results and celebrate overlaps.

Why it works:

Children learn that emotions carry vibration. By practicing symbolic sending and receiving, they validate their intuitive perceptions.

Telepathic Color Memory Path

This group game strengthens energetic memory and vibrational awareness.

How to do it:

1. Create a path of colored paper tiles on the floor (e.g., red, yellow, blue, green).

2. One child silently chooses a sequence of 3–4 tiles and walks it in their mind.

3. Their partner, without clues, attempts to walk the same sequence using intuition.

4. Switch roles and discuss how each person sensed the path (feeling, image, or knowing).

Why it works:

This practice blends color sensitivity with memory and intuition. It encourages children to notice how telepathic impressions come to them.

Intention Mandalas

A creative way to practice sending ideas through symbols and design.

How to do it:

1. Children create circular mandalas using natural objects, colors, or drawings that represent an idea (such as "kindness" or "focus").

2. Others walk around the mandala and describe what they sense.

Why it works:

Symbols bypass logic and carry vibration. Mandalas teach children that images can transmit energy and meaning nonverbally.

Thought Sketch Relay

This game turns mental images into shared drawings.

How to do it:

1. One child imagines a visual scene (e.g., a treehouse, glowing orb).

2. They silently "send" the image.

3. Others try to sketch what they received.

4. Compare and discuss patterns or similarities.

Why it works:

Children learn that thoughts can carry visual information. This strengthens both telepathy and observation skills.

Coherence Circle

A group practice for building collective harmony and trust.

How to do it:

1. Sit together in a circle with eyes closed.

2. Breathe slowly in rhythm as a group.

3. Each person silently sends a loving message into the circle.
4. After a few minutes, open your eyes and share how the room feels.

Why it works:

Group coherence amplifies energy. This practice creates stillness, harmony, and a felt sense of shared connection.

Toolbox Wrap-Up

These games and practices are more than fun activities—they are doorways into a deeper way of relating. Each exercise gives children permission to trust their subtle impressions and shows them that what they sense inside is real, valuable, and worth sharing.

Whether they are sketching a thought, weaving a mandala, or sitting together in a circle of silence, children learn that energy is as much a language as words. And parents, teachers, and peers learn alongside them that connection can be felt, not just spoken.

If you use even one or two of these practices consistently, you will notice a shift. Children become more confident, more compassionate, and more willing to share their inner world. Groups become calmer, more cooperative, and more attuned.

Telepathy is not a skill to master in one sitting. It is a rhythm to rediscover, a remembering. By returning to these simple practices, families and classrooms alike begin to reclaim the silent bonds of empathy, intuition, and trust that make communication whole again.

Invitation

You are not just teaching students to memorize facts; you are awakening their ability to feel truth, speak in silence, and know themselves as radiant creators. These schools are not far away. They begin with a single choice: to trust energy, honor intuition, and lead with love.

Whether you teach one child or an entire class, your presence becomes the tuning fork for a new world.

Transmission from Students in the Future

We remember what you have forgotten.
We listen in color,
we dream in light,
we build with sound.
Teach us, and we will teach you.
Together, we rise to re-sing the song of the world.

Up Next:

Before children speak with words, they speak with energy.
Before they explain, they transmit.

In the next chapter, we will step into the subtle, often overlooked ways children communicate through presence, sensation, gesture, rhythm, and silence. We will explore how intuition is expressed without language, how meaning can be felt rather than spoken, and how learning to listen beyond words allows us to receive what children are already sharing.

Chapter 10 invites us to slow down, soften our attention, and rediscover a language we once knew well—the language without words.

CHAPTER 10
The Language Without Words

In the gentle spaces between thought and speech, there exists a place where children still speak fluently. It is a language that does not rely on words, logic, or explanation. It is felt before it is understood. It is known before it is spoken.

This chapter is not about where children come from or what they may remember from elsewhere. It is about how they communicate **now**— through presence, energy, rhythm, gaze, movement, and stillness. Many children are not trying to send messages. They are simply being themselves, and in doing so, they transmit information constantly.

These are the Telepathic Ones: children who have not yet learned to silence their inner signal. Their messages are rarely verbal, yet they are unmistakably clear. They transmit through drawings, dreams, the steady gaze of their eyes, and the calm—or intensity—of their presence. They are part of a quiet revolution, reminding us that communication does not begin with language. It begins with awareness.

Messages Remembered and Received

Some of these children speak of other lifetimes, galaxies, or missions. Some simply radiate a vibration that shifts the energy in the room. They do not need to prove their knowing; it is felt. And when they communicate in ways we recognize, their insights are often surprisingly profound.

One child, during a quiet moment in a session, reached out and placed their hand gently over my heart. "Your light is tangled," they said, "but do not worry. The trees remember who you are. Just go outside and breathe

123

with them." That message was not random. It was precise. It unknotted a deep ache I had not realized I had been carrying.

That message was not random. It was exact. It released a deep ache I had not realized I was carrying. Nothing else needed to be said.

Another nonverbal boy I worked with would trace spirals on the ground every time I entered the room. When asked to draw what he sensed, he created detailed constellations and beams of light. Later, through symbols and gesture, he conveyed that he was sending calming energy into the land around us. When I asked how he knew how to do that, his response was simple:

"I just do."

Visions of Love and Energy

Many of these children communicate through color and feeling. One girl who had never spoken a word painted only in purple and gold. Her parents thought it was a coincidence until she began to gesture toward the sky every time a solar flare was due to arrive. "She's reading the sun," her mother whispered to me. I agreed.

Some children express visions of unity, of oneness. A six-year-old, after a quiet music session, once said: "When I play my heart music, I can feel the animals sleeping in the ground. The ants, the bears, even the tree roots. They all feel safe when I am singing with my bones."

Research from the HeartMath Institute supports this idea, showing that love and emotion are not only felt but also measurable as energetic frequencies. Their studies demonstrate that the rhythms of the heart can synchronize between people, confirming what these children so naturally display: love is vibration.

These are not fantasies. These are transmissions. Telepathy, for many of these children, is not a gift to be developed; it is a memory they have not yet forgotten.

My Husband's Earthquake Vision

When my husband was ten years old, he came to his parents and said there would be a big earthquake several months from that day. He gave them the date. They took him seriously. They moved all breakable and valuable items to safety. They mentally prepared and rehearsed what to do. Then, five months later, one day before the date he had predicted, a moderate earthquake struck. The epicenter was directly beneath their home.

And yet, nothing broke. Not a single fragile item was lost. His vision had prompted action that protected them. His ability to receive that future message through intuition or telepathic resonance made all the difference.

He shared with me that he felt the message arrive as a sense of urgency. Not panic, but a knowing. He did not hear a voice. He simply knew. He also felt that the information was given to him by benevolent beings watching over him, just like Beanie and Deany.

Who Were and Are Beanie and Deany?

During his childhood, my husband had two playmates named Beanie and Deany. These were not imaginary friends in the usual sense. To him, they were real beings who would call to him from outside, asking him to come out and play. They never came inside; they always waited outside, encouraging him to come play.

His parents accepted his playmates as part of his world. Each time he said, "I am going out to play with Beanie and Deany," they approved with no concern, questions, or comments as though they equally understood. An interesting side note is that when his dad first heard of them, he said there was no one with the name Beanie. He changed his tune when they moved to California and lived in a house built by a man named Beanie, who was the son of their sweet, grandmother-type neighbor.

These two companions would take him to a white room with no shadows, a place unlike any on Earth. The walls, the floors, and the ceiling were luminous and made of light. The corners were rounded and the walls smooth. In that space, they sat together on the floor, playing

125

board games, laughing, and sharing stories. But these were not just games. These were experiences rich with symbolism, lessons, and connection.

They told him stories about friendship, kindness, and empathy. They taught him through their games how to resolve conflict, how to be patient, and how to lead with the heart. They always emphasized love, care, and integrity. Looking back, he says he always knew they had a purpose: they were there to help him remain loving, caring, and kind throughout his life. In my opinion, they have succeeded.

Today, decades later, multiple psychics have confirmed that Beanie and Deany are still with him and he is still aware of their presence and asks them to help sometimes. They have never left. They are guides, allies, or perhaps even aspects of his higher consciousness. In any case, he regards them as real beings and understands they were assigned to him. He believes they could not be more willing or happier to be in his life and support his loving nature. They continue to protect and inform him, subtly guiding his life's direction.

These stories are not isolated. They are part of a global pattern where more and more children are arriving with inner memory fully intact.

Children as Natural Communicators

These stories are not isolated. More and more children arrive with a strong ability to sense subtle information and communicate without language.

Neuroscientist Stephen Porges, PhD, describes this capacity in his Polyvagal Theory: our nervous systems are wired for connection and safety long before words develop. Sensitive children simply reveal this wiring more openly.

Some communicate through dreams. Others through symbols or movement. Some appear to sense energetic shifts in environments or people without being taught how.

What makes these children different is not their ability to communicate—it is our ability to receive. The quieter we become, the more we can hear. The more we trust, the more they share.

Lessons from the Telepathic Ones

These children teach through presence, not performance.

They do not need to convince us of their truth. They simply radiate it.

And if we are willing to sit still, to feel instead of fixing, to observe without interpreting, we will receive more than words ever could convey.

They remind us:

Love is a vibration, not just a sentiment. Love, in their world, is not limited to emotion or affection. It is an energetic frequency. It can be sent and received, sensed and amplified. It is the harmonic resonance that binds all things.

Healing can happen without hands, only intention. These children intuitively understand that healing is a process of energy realignment. With focused intention and an open heart, they transmit frequencies that calm, soothe, and repair.

We are all connected through an unseen field of consciousness. This invisible matrix, sometimes called the Unified Field, the Akashic Field, or the Morphogenetic Field, connects every being to every other. These children navigate this field naturally, without instruction.

Memory is not bound to time. It lives in frequency. Rather than recalling events chronologically, they access memories encoded in vibration. This is why they can *remember* past lives, other realms, or galactic histories. They are not remembering the way adults do. They are tuning in.

Listening requires no ears.

Stillness is a frequency, not a pause.

Every child remembers the stars; they are just waiting for us to ask.

Remembering Ourselves

This chapter is not just about magical children. It is about all of us. We were all once like this.

We were once the ones who spoke with color, felt in patterns, and knew in pulses.

The Telepathic Ones are not rare. They are just the ones who stayed open.

Let us open again.
Let us listen.
Let us remember.

Science Note

Research in heart-field communication and intuitive development supports the idea that many children are already attuned to invisible forms of intelligence. The HeartMath Institute has shown that the electromagnetic rhythms of the heart can synchronize between individuals, especially during moments of emotional resonance. Neuroscientist Dr. Stephen Porges' *Polyvagal Theory* suggests that our nervous systems are wired for connection, even beyond verbal cues.

Meanwhile, decades of experiments by Dr. Dean Radin at the *Institute of Noetic Sciences* provide rigorous evidence that intuition and telepathy can be measured. His research on presentiment shows that the human body responds to emotional images and events seconds before they occur, suggesting awareness beyond time. Radin's double-blind Ganzfeld telepathy experiments reveal that people can send and receive images and impressions across distance at statistically significant levels. His studies in entangled minds point to a deep, underlying field of consciousness where information travels without physical contact.

Together, these findings affirm what many sensitive children already demonstrate: that knowing can arrive without sound, memory is not bound by time, and love can speak without words.

Practitioner Prompt

The next time a child says something that seems unusual, symbolic, or surreal, pause. Ask yourself, "What if this is real?" Record the moment. Sit with it. These messages are not meant to impress you. They are meant to awaken you.

Telepathy Toolbox

These practices are designed to help children (and the adults who love them) share messages in simple, symbolic, and energetic ways. They strengthen nonverbal connection, trust, and sensitivity to the unseen fields of communication that surround us.

Crystal Grid Messages

This practice uses crystals as carriers of silent messages.

How to do it:

1. Choose five to seven crystals or rocks.
2. Let your child intuitively place them into a pattern.
3. Sit with the layout in silence and ask inwardly: *"What is this pattern saying?"*
4. Share your impressions aloud or draw them.

Why it works:

Crystals amplify energy. By arranging them intuitively, children create symbolic messages that can be felt and interpreted, validating nonverbal communication.

Silent Stone Circles

This group exercise helps children learn how intention can be stored and sensed.

How to do it:

1. Each person holds a small stone while sitting in a circle.
2. Close your eyes and silently "send" a thought or feeling into the stone.
3. Pass the stones around the circle.
4. When you receive one, sense what it carries, then share what came through.

Why it works:

Stones act as simple vessels for intention. Passing them builds trust and shows that thoughts and feelings can travel through objects as well as through people.

Telepathic Story Stones

This activity turns natural objects into tools for silent storytelling.

How to do it:

1. Gather natural objects such as a leaf, shell, feather, or bead.
2. Without speaking, choose one and send a silent "story" using only that object.
3. The partner describes what they received.
4. Switch roles and repeat.

Why it works:

Objects become symbols that carry energetic meaning. This strengthens symbolic thinking, telepathic expression, and intuitive listening.

Light Signature Drawing

This exercise helps children express how their energy feels in the moment.

How to do it:

1. Ask your child to imagine what their "light" looks like today— its color, movement, or shape.

2. Each person silently senses the other's *light*.

3. Draw what you felt from the other's field.

4. Compare drawings and discuss feelings.

Why it works:

Children learn to notice and express their energy field in creative ways. Comparing drawings validates shared impressions and builds confidence in subtle sensing.

Message from the Trees

This practice invites children to receive wisdom directly from nature.

How to do it:

1. Sit quietly under a tree with your child.

2. Place your hand on the trunk or ground in silence.

3. Ask inwardly: *"What message do you have for us today?"*

4. After a few minutes, draw or speak what you received.

Why it works:

Trees hold steady vibrational fields that children often sense naturally. This exercise deepens their relationship with nature and shows them that communication is possible with all living beings.

Toolbox Wrap-Up

These activities are not about performance or accuracy—they are about presence. Each game or practice invites children to remember that their silent language is valid and trustworthy. The more you listen, draw, and share, the more fluent this language becomes.

Over time, you will discover that these "games" are actually doorways into the deeper memory of who we are: connected, intuitive, and already communicating beyond words.

Invitation

What if these children are not here to be corrected, but to remind us how to listen?

What if their silence is not absence, but language?

This chapter invites you to soften your attention and widen your field. You do not need to be psychic. You do not need to interpret.

You only need to notice

Transmission from the Telepathic Ones

We do not speak to your ears.
We speak to your listening.

When you quiet your field,
we are already here.

Up Next:

Not all memories come easily. In the next chapter, we will explore what happens when intuition is blocked, memory is suppressed, and children begin to forget who they are and how we can gently help them remember.

PART THREE

The Remembering

All great achievements of science must start from
intuitive knowledge.

— Unknown

CHAPTER 11

Remembering What You Never Lost

Long before we had words, we had knowing. Before language took form in our throats, it rose in our fields. Telepathy is not futuristic; it is ancient, woven into the fabric of every child and forgotten by most adults. But it can be remembered.

Why You Once Had It, and How to Reclaim It

Every human being is born with subtle communication abilities. As infants, we communicated through resonance and energy. We read the emotional climate of a room before we could understand its vocabulary. We responded to facial micro-expressions, touch, color, and tone. These are remnants of our natural telepathic wiring.

Over time, as logic and language took dominance, the "listening ear" of intuition and the "seeing eye" of inner vision were dismissed as imaginary. But those senses are still present. They can be reactivated.

Bruce Lipton, Ph.D., in *Biology of Belief: Unleashing the Power of Consciousness, Matter, and Miracles*, explains how our thoughts influence our biology. His groundbreaking research shows that beliefs are not just stored in the brain but ripple through the body, affecting every cell. When we believe we are intuitive, that belief can help reactivate dormant abilities, including telepathy.

This scientific validation makes it easier to trust what we sense but cannot see.

Dr. Bradley Nelson's work with the Emotion Code® and Belief Code® supports this as well. He teaches that trapped emotions and faulty subconscious beliefs can block our innate gifts. By identifying and releasing these blocks, often using muscle-testing and magnetic clearing, individuals report a return to clarity, intuition, and even psychic communication.

Guided Visualization to Recall Telepathic Memories from Childhood

Find a quiet space. Close your eyes and breathe deeply. Visualize yourself as a child in a wall-less room of soft light and warmth. You feel safe, held, connected.

Now, remember a time before words. You may recall a feeling of knowing something before it happened. A sense that you and a friend understood each other without speaking. A dream that came true. Let it arise.

Ask yourself gently: What do I know now that I had forgotten?

Rest in this memory. Feel its texture. Let the sensation of preverbal communication wash over you. Trust what arises, even if it seems subtle.

One woman shared that after doing eye-gazing with her teenage son for just two minutes, they both began crying, not from sadness, but from a wordless, mutual recognition. "It felt like we would met again for the first time," she said. "Without needing to explain who we were."

Practices to Rebuild the Inner *Listening Ear* and *Seeing Eye*

Reawakening your telepathic nature involves retraining your attention. Here are some simple daily practices:

Inner Listening:

Spend five minutes a day focusing on your heartbeat or breath. Then shift your awareness to the space around you. What do you sense without sound?

Eye Gazing:

Sit with a partner and look into each other's eyes without speaking for two to three minutes. Exchange feelings, images, or thoughts silently.

Symbol Interpretation:

Begin to pay attention to recurring symbols in your dreams or daily life. These are part of your soul's language.

Nature Communication:

Go into nature and attune to a tree, plant, or animal. Quiet your mind and ask a question silently. Wait for a sense, feeling, image, or idea in return.

Partner Exercises, Group Experiments, and Quiet Intuition Strengthening

Intuition blooms in community. Here are some practices that help:

Image Sending:

One person thinks of a simple shape, color, or object. The other writes down or draws what comes to mind. Compare results.

Dream Seeding:

Before sleep, two partners agree to meet in dreams. They hold an image in their minds and journal what happens. Compare notes.

Vibe Check:

In group settings, pause and have everyone sense the energy in the room. Compare descriptions. This increases sensitivity and validation.

Silent Storytelling:

A partner creates a short silent story using only facial expression and body language. The other intuitively writes what the story was about.

Clearing with Frequency-Based Support

Clearing Blocks:

Belief, Trauma, Skepticism, and Distraction

The biggest barriers to telepathic reconnection are not lack of ability but internal interference. These include:

Belief Blocks:

If you were told it was imaginary, evil, or fake, your subconscious may have buried the gift. Affirm: It is safe to know. It is safe to see. It is safe to remember.

Trauma:

Emotional wounds can distort intuitive signals. Healing trauma helps clear the signal.

Neurobiologist Dr. Candace Pert's discovery of neuropeptides, which she called the *molecules of emotion*, supports this idea. Her research shows that memory and intuition are stored throughout the body as well as in the brain. When emotional blocks are released, access to these inner senses often returns with surprising clarity.

Skepticism:

Healthy discernment is good. But cynicism closes the door. Replace doubt with curiosity.

Distraction:

Constant digital noise suppresses the inner senses. Build daily time for stillness.

Support from Broad Spectrum DeTOX

Many adults seeking to reawaken their inner senses have found that physical detoxification can accelerate the process. This is partly because the pineal gland, our intuitive antenna, is often calcified due to fluoride, toxins, and heavy metals.

Broad Spectrum DeTOX offers a powerful tool for this journey. Participants have reported increased vivid dreaming, intuition, and clarity after using this system.

If you are on the path to reclaiming your telepathic nature, this is a valuable support. Pair physical detox with spiritual practice for accelerated reawakening. There is more information on this in Appendix H- When Telepathy Seems Lost.

The Role of the Field

Author Gregg Braden refers to *The Divine Matrix*, a term synonymous with the field of consciousness that connects all living things.

This *matrix* is not fiction; it is measurable and real. He explains that our thoughts, beliefs, and emotions influence this unified field and can shape reality. Lynne McTaggart, in her book *The Field*, documents scientific studies proving that human intention can affect matter and energy. She calls this invisible web *the field*. It is often referred to as the *zero-point field*. It is a quantum sea of energy and information. Her research shows that our thoughts can travel across distance, suggesting that telepathy is simply interaction within this interconnected field.

Biophysicist Dr. Beverly Rubik expands this understanding with her research on the *biofield*, the subtle energy matrix that surrounds the body. She suggests the biofield may be the very interface through which telepathy and nonlocal communication occur.

How to Work with the Field

This field is not reserved for mystics or scientists. It is accessible to anyone willing to learn. That is why Susan V Whittaker wrote the book, *Diving Deep Into the Ocean of the Mind: A Dowser's Guide for Searching, Empowerment, and Elevating Your Subconscious Mind*. It teaches how to use dowsing tools to explore the field, uncover limiting beliefs, and make empowered choices.

Dowsing allows access to subconscious truth—often buried under programming and fear. Through charts and focused questioning, you can train yourself to tune into the field with precision and clarity. This is the same field where telepathy lives.

Dowsing is a form of telepathy: between you and your subconscious, your higher self, or the field itself.

This chapter is your invitation to remember. Not to learn something new, but to return to what was always yours. The language of energy. The pulse of intuition. The memory behind your words. You are still telepathic. You always were. Emerging research in consciousness studies confirms that intuitive knowing can be cultivated—even after years of

141

suppression. Dr. Judith Orloff, a psychiatrist specializing in empathic sensitivity, has shown that intuition is not only real but often reactivates through healing and inner stillness.

Science Note

Science across multiple fields confirms what many are remembering: intuition is not lost, only buried. Bruce Lipton's research in epigenetics shows that beliefs shape biology and can activate dormant intuitive abilities. Dr. Bradley Nelson demonstrates how clearing trapped emotions restores clarity and connection. Gregg Braden and Lynne McTaggart describe the unified *field*, an invisible matrix of energy, where intention and communication travel across space and time.

Dr. Beverly Rubik's *biofield* research and Dr. Candace Pert's discovery of the *molecules of emotion* suggest that intuition is not only neural but cellular, woven through the body itself. And psychiatrist Dr. Judith Orloff affirms that intuition often reawakens through healing and empathic sensitivity. Together, their work shows that telepathy is not new; it is the ancient language of energy waiting to be remembered.

Practitioner Prompt

As a caregiver, coach, or therapist, have you ever known the truth of a client's struggle before they said a word?

Begin tracking these moments, not as coincidence, but confirmation.

Let intuition become part of your clinical notes.

It might just become your most reliable tool.

Reflection Prompt: Have you noticed yourself intuitively knowing a client's answer before it was spoken?

How might you shift your practice to honor these nonverbal communications more directly?

Telepathy Toolbox

These simple tools help reawaken your inner senses and rebuild nonverbal connection with others, with nature, and with the field itself. They are designed to be gentle doorways, not pressured practices.

Repeat group exercises like dream seeding and silent storytelling to sharpen reception. Wait for the first feeling, word, or image that arises. Trust it.

Soul-to-Soul Journaling

Build energetic dialogue across time and identity.

How to do it:

1. Write a letter to your child, partner, or even your younger self.
2. Then switch roles and "channel" a reply as if you are that person (or your younger self) writing back.
3. Continue the exchange for a few minutes, letting intuition guide the words.

Why it works:

This practice bypasses linear thought and allows the subconscious to speak. Children and adults alike discover that telepathy is not only possible with others but within the many layers of the self.

Symbol Tuning

Use symbols to track your energy over time.

143

How to do it:

1. At the end of the day, pause and ask: *"What symbol represents my energy right now?"*

2. Draw it on paper without judgment.

3. Write one or two words about its feeling or message.

4. Keep a log so you can notice patterns over days and weeks.

Why it works:

Symbols are the language of the subconscious. Keeping a running log trains you to recognize your own energetic patterns and strengthens intuitive interpretation.

Tree Whispering

Learn to receive wisdom directly from nature.

How to do it:

1. Choose one tree in your yard, neighborhood, or park.

2. Sit quietly with it once a week. Place your hand on its trunk or simply lean against it.

3. Ask a silent question and wait for impressions, images, or feelings.

4. Record what arises in a journal—especially any dreams or shifts afterward.

Why it works:

Trees hold steady, grounding vibrations. Returning to the same tree builds relationship and shows that communication extends beyond humans.

Frequency Anchoring

Use sound to reawaken memory and intuitive awareness.

How to do it:

1. Choose a tone—hum, sing, or play a tuning fork.

2. Focus on how your body feels as you make or hear the sound.

3. Repeat the same tone daily for one week.

4. Journal any memories, images, or sensations that arise.

Why it works:

Sound bypasses logic and travels directly into the body's memory field. Anchoring a specific tone helps awaken stored impressions and strengthens your sensitivity to vibrational language.

Toolbox Wrap-Up

These practices remind us that telepathy is not limited to mind-to-mind images. It flows through symbols, sound, memory, and nature. Each exercise invites you to slow down and trust the subtle responses.

The more you record, draw, and reflect, the more fluent this inner language becomes. Over time, you will see that intuition is not fragile or rare; it is reliable, ever-present, and waiting to be remembered. Telepathy is not about trying harder; it is about creating space for the truth you already carry to speak again.

Invitation

You were never meant to lose this language.

It only went quiet while the world got loud.

Now, with each breath of stillness, each moment of trust, each spark of curiosity, it begins to return.

Telepathy is not beyond you; it is within you.

Let this be your remembering. Let this be your return.

Transmission from the Remembering Ones

We are not lost,
we are dormant within you.
Each still breath stirs the memory.
Each brave "yes" calls us closer.
The field is not elsewhere.
It is you. Awakened.

Up Next

In Chapter 12, we will turn our attention to what children have been hearing, and saying, all along. We will meet the Telepathic Ones: children who remember past lives, speak in symbols, and carry messages from realms beyond logic. Their words, drawings, and silent *knowings* invite us to believe not just in possibility, but in the continuity of consciousness itself.

Soul Memory and the Ones Who Remember

Chapter 11 reminded us how to rebuild the inner listening ear.
This chapter reveals what sometimes rises into awareness when we do.

There is a quiet revolution blooming—a chorus rising from children who remember more than this lifetime alone. In their drawings, dreams, spontaneous statements, and moments of startling clarity, they deliver transmissions that feel older than language. These are not learned ideas. They are memories carried forward. These are the Ones Who Remember.

Children Who Remember

Some children arrive with memory unusually accessible. They speak of past lives, of floating above their bodies, of conversations with angels or star beings. Their memories are not metaphor. They arrive with specificity, emotion, and coherence—as frequency echoes that surface through the veil of time.

One child spoke of choosing her parents before birth, selecting them from a celestial library of glowing orbs. Another drew blueprints of a ship that closely resembled NASA schematics, though she had never seen one before. Others describe colors without names and places that shimmer between dimensions.

Even nonverbal children sometimes communicate remembered knowing. Through their eyes, hands, or focused silence, they transmit love, fear, and certainty. One boy sat beneath a tree each day and hummed a melody that calmed birds and drew butterflies to his shoulders. Another girl placed her hands on her mother's stomach and communicated inwardly, "The baby is healthy now." That same day, a long-feared medical test came back clear.

Shared Memory Beyond Words

One experience from my own life left me both stunned and deeply confirmed.

At a spiritual event, I was drawn without explanation to a lapis lazuli stone sold by a man I had never met. That night, I dreamed of him. We stood in an immense cave filled with crystals so large we could not join hands and reach around them. He plucked the crystals with his fingers, and they sang—clear, resonant, and alive.

I woke and described the dream to my husband in vivid detail: what we wore, the texture of the cave, the tones of the singing stones.

The next day, the same man walked into our booth and approached my husband. Without prompting, he said, "Sir, I had a dream about your wife last night." He then described the same cave. The same massive crystals. The same act of plucking them into song.

Word for word. Image for image.

We had entered the same memory field. It was more than coincidence and more than imagination. It was a reminder that memory does not always belong to one mind—and that sometimes, two souls remember together.

Notable Cases of Childhood Memory

Perhaps the most thoroughly documented modern case is that of **James Leininger**, an American boy who began having vivid nightmares at age two. He screamed about a plane on fire and a "little man who could not get out." He named his aircraft carrier "Natoma," spoke of a pilot friend named "Jack Larsen," and said he had been shot down by the Japanese during World War II.

His parents eventually traced his statements to **James Huston Jr.**, a Navy pilot killed at Iwo Jima. James correctly identified aircraft, locations, and fellow servicemen from a war fought decades before his birth. Many of his statements were recorded before Huston was identified. His case remains one of the strongest Western examples of childhood reincarnation memory.

Another American child astonished family and observers with innate musical mastery. Given a fiddle, he played not only familiar songs but compositions unique to **Bob Wills**, the King of Western Swing. His technique, timing, and tone were so precise that musicians who had worked with Wills believed the child carried his musical memory forward. This was not imitation. It was memory expressing itself through the body.

Shanti Devi, born in 1930s India, began speaking at age four of her home in Mathura. She named her husband, described her death in childbirth, and led investigators to her former town. There, she recognized her previous family and identified where money had been buried in the home. Although the cache was empty—her widower had already taken it—every other detail was verified. Her case drew the attention of **Mahatma Gandhi** and remains foundational in reincarnation research.

Real Stories from the Field

These stories are not isolated. They form a global pattern, spanning cultures and centuries.

A teacher in Oregon shared how a seven-year-old student once approached her and said, "Your brother forgives you," though the teacher had never mentioned his death to anyone.

An energy healer recalled a young client who placed crystals around a room in a precise grid and said, "Now the energy will not hurt anymore."

A speech therapist observed that a nonverbal child began improving only after being allowed to communicate through color and symbol rather than speech drills.

In third-century China, a child asked his nanny for a gold ring he used to play with. When told he never had one, he walked to a mulberry tree and pulled it from the ground. It had belonged to a neighbor's deceased child.

In the 1800s Syrian Druze community, a boy claimed to have been a wealthy man in Damascus. He guided his family to the city, identified his widow, and revealed where money had been buried in his former home. It was found exactly as described.

In 1920s India, **Vishwa Nath** recalled a former life with such clarity that investigators confirmed his statements under the name **Bishen Chand Kapoor**, later reinvestigated by **Dr. Ian Stevenson**.

149

Another case involved **Savitri Devi Pathak**, who remembered burying money near a drain in a previous life. Though the money was gone, the accuracy of her location was verified.

What the Children Remind Us

These children are not trying to become telepathic.
They are trying not to forget.

You were once like them—whole, tuned, and receptive. You still are.

They remind us:

- Love is vibration, not just sentiment.
- Memory can move through frequency rather than time.
- Healing follows intention.
- Pure intent amplifies effect.
- Consciousness is shared, not contained.

Gregg Braden describes this interconnected field as the **Divine Matrix**—an intelligent web linking all things. **Lynne McTaggart**, in *The Field*, echoes this understanding, describing consciousness as a shared resonance rather than an isolated function.

When a child knows something they "should not," it is not because they imagined it. It is because memory lives beyond the boundaries we were taught to accept.

Memory is not bound to time.
It lives in frequency.

Science Note

Emerging research in brain-heart coherence shows that when the brain and heart are in sync, intuitive insights become stronger and more reliable. This is not just theory; it is measurable. Gregg Braden's concept of the *Divine Matrix* proposes that we live within a field of consciousness where thoughts, emotions, and memories can travel across space and time. And Dr. Candace Pert's work on neuropeptides, *molecules of emotion*, reveals that intuition is not just in the mind; it is felt and processed throughout the body. When children remember what adults forget, they are not imagining; they are remembering through the field.

Practitioner Prompt

When a child says something mysterious, metaphorical, or impossible, pause. Ask: "What if they are remembering something I have forgotten?"

Do not dismiss it. Record it. Reflect on it. You might be receiving a message, not a story.

Telepathy Toolbox

These activities help children explore memory, imagination, and identity as doorways into telepathic awareness. Sometimes what seems like *pretend* is actually a remembered truth. Treat these games with lightness and curiosity, letting your child lead.

Soul Memory Match
Explore memories through symbolic images.

How to do it:

1. Print or draw 6–10 simple scenes (ocean, mountain, starry sky, forest, temple, spaceship).
2. Lay them out and invite your child to choose the one that feels *familiar*.
3. Ask: *"What do you remember?"*
4. Record or draw their responses together.

Why it works:

Children often respond strongly to symbolic landscapes. These scenes can unlock past-life echoes or inner stories waiting to be told.

Star Map Drawing

Use drawing to access memories of other skies.

How to do it:

1. Invite your child to close their eyes and imagine looking at the night sky—not Earth's, but one from *somewhere else.*
2. Ask them to draw the stars, shapes, or symbols they see.
3. Share impressions: *"Where might this sky be?"*

Why it works:

Children naturally carry archetypal memories of the cosmos. Drawing helps anchor impressions that words may not capture.

Past Life Echo Objects

Let objects become storytellers of hidden memory.

How to do it:

1. Gather small mysterious objects (old key, photo, trinket, coin).
2. Hold one at a time and say: *"If this came from another life, what story would it tell?"*
3. Let your child share freely—through words, drawings, or gestures.

Why it works:

Objects act as energetic triggers. Even when it feels like imagination, the stories often echo deeper memory.

Portal Walk

Step into different lifetimes through play.

How to do it:

1. Create three to four "portals" using chairs, hoops, or cloths.
2. Invite your child to silently step through each one.
3. After each step, ask: *"Who are you here? What do you feel, see, or remember?"*
4. Let them describe or act it out.

Why it works:

Movement activates imagination and memory. Portals help children shift states and access layers of identity.

Who Am I Today?

Honor shifting identities as windows into memory.

How to do it:

1. Each morning, ask your child to pause and tune in.
2. Ask: *"Who am I today?"* and let them answer without logic.
3. Accept roles like healer, explorer, star-child, indigo-child, or lion-hearted one.
4. Follow up: *"And what do you remember?"*
5. Write their answers in a journal.

Why it works:

Children experience identity fluidly. By validating their spontaneous responses, you open a safe space for remembered wisdom to surface.

Toolbox Wrap-Up

These practices blur the line between memory and imagination, exactly where intuition lives. What children describe may sound like stories, but beneath the stories are often truths carried in the soul.

When you invite them to draw star maps, step through portals, or hold "mysterious" objects, you affirm that their inner knowing is real and worth listening to. Over time, these playful rituals help children keep alive the sense that they are more than this moment—they are timeless beings with wisdom to share.

Invitation

Speak the Language of the Soul.

This book is not just a manual.
It is a mirror.

To the part of you that already knows.
To the voice that grows louder in stillness.
To the eye that sees in dreams.
To the ear that hears through the heart.

The Ones Who Remember are not confined to childhood. They are present wherever memory is allowed to surface.

You were once one of them.
You still are.

The question is not whether telepathy is real.
The question is whether you are willing to remember.

Transmission from the Telepathic Ones

We never left.
We live in the spaces you forgot to listen to.
In dreams. In glances. In sudden knowing.

You knew us before words.
Now you are learning to trust the remembering again.

Up Next:

As the Telepathic Ones awaken something deep within, stir memory, resonance, or a quiet knowing, we can begin learning how to help children shape the field around them with intention, frequency, and love.

In the next chapter, we will move from receiving messages to creating them. We will explore how children can program the invisible by infusing the energies of thoughts and intentions into water, crystals, and the world.

CHAPTER 13

Programming the Invisible

Children are not only receivers; they are creators.

It begins with a thought.

A feeling.

A spark in the chest.

A vision held in the heart.

Children naturally know that their world responds to them. Watch them whisper to a toy, place a stone on a windowsill like a ritual, or line up items with mysterious precision. They are remembering what most adults forgot: that the world listens.

We live in a universe that responds to vibration. When we teach children to work with energy intentionally, not just to feel it, but to shape it, we empower them to become active creators of their own reality.

What Is Programming?

There is a sacred act of programming the invisible that can be taught to Children

1. **Choose a focus.** Ask: *"What do you want this to carry or remind you of?"* (peace, courage, love, safety, etc.).

2. **Add feeling.** Close your eyes together and really feel that quality in the body (e.g., imagine peace as a blue wave, courage as a golden flame).

3. **Send the intention.** Place hands on the object (or imagine surrounding the room/yourself with light). Say: *"I am filling you with ___."*

4. **Seal it.** Take one deep breath and imagine the feeling "clicking in," like pressing save on a computer.

5. **Test it.** Invite the child to hold the water, crystal, or drawing and ask: *"What do you feel now?"* Encourage them to notice sensations, emotions, or shifts.

Why This Matters

Programming teaches children they are not powerless. They learn that:

1. Intention changes energy.
2. Emotions carry frequency.
3. They can shape their environment instead of only reacting to it.

This is not about "teaching magic." It is about teaching mastery: the ability to consciously choose, send, and hold a vibration. Over time, children learn that they can walk into any situation, a classroom, a challenge, a moment of fear—and program themselves with the frequency they most need.

The Language of Intention

Intention is energy plus direction.

It is the message you send into the field.

The clearer the message, the stronger the response.

You can teach this to a three-year-old with a stuffed bear:

"Tell the bear how you want it to feel today."

You can teach it to a ten-year-old with a water bottle:

"Hold it in your hands and think of something kind. Drink it."

Or teach it to a teenager:

"Breathe your intention into this drawing. What does it want to become?"

They will remember. They always do.

Consciousness Confirmed

The author had an experience at the *Extraordinary Tesla Tech Conference* (2023) that illustrates the potential and practicality of these mental programming activities when she came across a technology that confirmed what she had always known intuitively: consciousness is not contained; it is creative.

A gentleman was demonstrating a handheld biofeedback device with a line of 12 small green LED lights lined up in a row about three inches long. This device did not respond to sound, light, heat, or motion; it responded only to thought.

When the machine was on, seven lights were off and five LEDs were on and formed a group. By the lights turning on and off, it appeared that the group of five lights was moving back and forth. As I watched, the group never split apart. Sometimes the group would move irregularly. Sometimes it moved from side to side and sometimes it would pause and then move in either direction. This puzzled me. The group had no apparent pattern or cause. The inventor smiled and told me the lights responded to thought.

With quiet focus, participants were asked to move the group of shining lights from one side to the other, using only their mind. It was not magic. It was measured intention, interacting with machinery designed to detect the smallest energetic shifts of mental energy.

The author, as one of very few, easily moved the lights; not through willpower or force, but through presence. The machine registered her consciousness as a field that could influence, direct, and harmonize with the device itself. The little group of lights would shift back and forth from side to side, although the author was only moving them to the right. The puzzling "ping-pong game" was revealed when the inventor laughed and admitted he was moving the group to the left each time she moved them to the right. He praised her and said she was one of very few who could do it.

What moved for me was not just the lights; it was the boundary of what I believed was possible. And now, perhaps, yours too. Every time the lights moved, someone was directing them through intention.

You have now walked through the remembering, chapter by chapter, frequency by frequency.

You have seen what lives behind the silence.

And now, it is no longer just your child who is telepathic.

You are.

You are a translator of light, a listener of dreams, a keeper of soul language. What comes next will not be found in the next page, but in the next moment when your child speaks without speaking, and you understand them completely.

Tools Children Can Program

Programming works best when children choose their own tools and lead the process. Their intuition already knows what each object or ritual wants to become. Your role is to guide gently, then step back and let them discover.

These activities help children explore emotions, intention, education and shape the environment around them, using consciousness and telepathic awareness.

Turn crystals into helpers and companions.

How to do it:
1. Ask: *"What does this crystal want to help you with today?"*
2. Let your child hold it in their hand.
3. Have them breathe in a color or word that matches the quality (e.g., "blue calm," "golden courage").

Why it works:
Crystals hold vibration easily. Pairing them with breath and color allows children to feel their intention flowing into the stone.

Water

Transform a glass of water into energetic medicine.

How to do it:
1. Pour a glass of water.
2. Ask: *"Can you make this water feel brave?"*

3. Blow gently, hum, or sing into it.

4. Drink slowly and reflect: *"How does it feel now?"*

Why it works:

Water is a perfect carrier of frequency. Children can sense subtle changes and begin to understand how intention shifts matter.

Stones or Shells

Everyday objects can become pocket charms.

How to do it:

1. Invite your child to choose a stone or shell.

2. Ask: *"What job will this stone do for you?"* (e.g., "help me feel safe," "remind me to be kind").

3. Let them keep it in a pocket or backpack.

Why it works:

Assigning a "job" to an object teaches children that energy can be stored and carried. The object becomes a touchstone for reassurance and focus.

Drawings & Mandalas

Use art as a frequency anchor.

How to do it:

1. Ask your child: *"Draw how you want tomorrow to feel."*

2. Let them create freely with colors and shapes.

3. Hang the drawing on the wall or near the bed.

Why it works:

Images hold intention. Displaying a drawing turns it into a visual reminder of the feeling they want to live in.

Color Codes

Turn colors into vibrational markers.

How to do it:

1. Together, assign meanings: red = strong, blue = calm, yellow = happy, etc.

2. Use stickers, ribbons, or markers in those colors to decorate their belongings.

Why it works:

Colors speak directly to the subconscious. This practice creates an easy, everyday coding system for emotional support.

Daily Programming Rituals

Small acts become powerful when repeated. These rituals show children how to weave programming into ordinary life.

Morning Light Programming

How to do it:

1. Place hands over the heart.

2. Say aloud: "I choose to feel ____ today."

3. Breathe the word into the hands, then touch backpack, shoes, or forehead to "charge" them.

Why it works:

Starting the day with intention sets the tone and teaches children that they can choose their vibration.

Bedtime Beam

How to do it:

1. Imagine a golden light above the bed.

2. Let it pour down gently over the body.

3. Ask: *"What do you want this light to bring you while you sleep?"*

Why it works:
The dream state is open to suggestion. A bedtime beam turns sleep into healing and memory integration.

Lunchtime Charging

How to do it:
1. Place both hands over food or drink.
2. Silently say: "Thank you. I charge you with ___."
3. Eat or drink with awareness.

Why it works:
This ritual teaches gratitude while reinforcing that nourishment carries frequency as well as nutrients.

Hand Activation

How to do it:
1. Rub palms together until warm.
2. Say: "These are my magic hands."
3. Invite your child to gently send energy into a plant, pet, or pillow.

Why it works:
Children learn that their minds and hands are natural transmitters of energy. This builds confidence and playfulness around their ability to affect the world.

Programming Wrap-Up
By programming their world, children begin to understand that their thoughts and feelings are powerful tools. Whether it is water, crystals, drawings, or daily rituals, each practice reinforces that energy responds to intention and their thoughts can become manifested around them.

This is not about "doing magic tricks." It is about giving children mastery, the ability to shift their own state and shape the world around them with love, courage, and clarity. Over time, these small acts become a way of living, reminding them that they are creators, not just observers, in their lives.

Energy Programming Is Measurable

What we call *programming* is the deliberate use of intention and emotion to affect the structure and behavior of matter. This might sound mystical, but science has already caught up.

Masaru Emoto, a Japanese researcher, became famous for photographing frozen water crystals after exposing them to words, music, and focused intention. Water exposed to "love" formed beautiful, symmetrical patterns. Water labeled with "hate" formed distorted, chaotic ones.

Veda Austin, a contemporary water researcher, continues this work with ice glyphs, showing that water responds to thoughts, images, and even memories. Children can repeat her experiments at home by freezing small bowls of water after silently "sending" a feeling into them.

Even rice experiments support this. In countless demonstrations, jars of cooked rice labeled with negative words like "stupid" or "hate" rot faster than those labeled with love. It is not the ink; it is the intention.

The author's book *The Complete Guide to Crystal Therapy: For the Body, Mind, and Spirit – Volumes 1 & 2*, provides a full methodology for working with crystals, including how to program them with specific intentions for the body, mind, or spirit. Crystals, like water, are receptive; they hold frequency and relay it over time.

This chapter builds upon that work: children do not need to wait to become adults to access this wisdom. They can begin programming objects, water, and their environment with healing frequencies, now, joyfully and intuitively.

Practitioner Prompt

Invite a child to choose a small object: a rock, a coin, a button.

Ask them to hold it and silently think of a feeling they want it to carry.

Then, trade objects so each can try to sense what feeling was programmed into it.

Reflect: "How did your body know?"

Telepathy Toolbox

These playful practices teach children that thoughts, feelings, and intentions can be sent, received, and shaped. They make telepathy visible and tangible, helping families experience the power of energy in everyday life.

Thoughtform Toss

Play catch with energy instead of a ball.

How to do it:

1. Imagine holding a ball of energy in your hands (e.g., "safety," "sunlight").
2. Pretend to toss it gently to your child.
3. When they "catch" it, ask them to describe what they felt.
4. Switch roles and repeat.

Why it works:

Children quickly realize that feelings and images can be transmitted without words. It builds confidence in their ability to sense energy.

Programmed Ice

Freeze an intention into form.

How to do it:

1. Fill a small bowl or tray with water.
2. Hold it together and silently send a word, symbol, or feeling into it.
3. Freeze the water.
4. Once frozen, photograph or observe the ice patterns.
5. Reflect on what message or shape appeared.

Why it works:

Water holds memory. This practice gives a visual confirmation that intention leaves an imprint.

Glow Stone Activation

Turn a glowing object into a nighttime ally.

How to do it:

1. Give your child a glow-in-the-dark stone.
2. Invite them to breathe in courage, then "send" that courage into the stone.
3. Place it under their pillow at night.
4. Remind them it is still working even when it is not glowing.

Why it works:

Children learn that programming lasts beyond what they can see, reinforcing trust in unseen energy.

Intention Jars

Collect and amplify family wishes.

How to do it:

1. Provide slips of paper and pens.
2. Write simple intentions such as "I want to feel more joy" or "I send love to Grandma."
3. Place the notes in a jar.
4. Shake the jar gently and set it near a candle or window.

Why it works:

Writing focuses the mind. Grouping intentions in one place magnifies them, showing children that energy grows when shared.

Crystal Charging Circle

Build a family altar of love and wishes.

How to do it:

1. Arrange crystals, drawings, or meaningful objects in a small circle or on a cloth.
2. Sit together around the circle.
3. Close your eyes, place hands over your hearts, and beam love or light into the center.
4. Add or change objects as intentions evolve.

Why it works:

Children see that energy can be gathered, focused, and shared. The altar becomes a physical reminder of connection and care.

Feel the Room Game

Tune into and shift the energy of a space.

How to do it:

1. Ask everyone: *"What does this room feel like right now?"*

2. Then ask: *"What do we want it to feel like?"*
3. Close your eyes together.
4. Breathe in the new feeling and imagine it filling the room.

Why it works:

This teaches children that spaces hold energy and that they have the power to shift the atmosphere with intention.

Toolbox Wrap-Up

These practices show children that energy responds to thought, feeling, and play. Whether they are tossing a ball of sunlight, programming a crystal, or changing the atmosphere of a room, they learn that their inner world has a direct impact on the outer one.

By turning intention into games, you normalize telepathy as a living skill. Over time, children begin to trust that their presence and focus matter, that they can program, shape, and brighten their world with love.

Invitation

Children are already working with energy.

The question is: are we teaching them to do it consciously?

When a child learns that their thoughts can soothe, protect, inspire, or heal, they begin to understand their power. Not a power over others, but a partnership with the field.

They stop asking, "What can I get?"

And start asking, "What can I create?"

Transmission from the Field

You were never meant to feel powerless.

Everything responds to your tone, your tears, your tenderness.

Even now, the room bends gently toward your heart.

168

We remember the moment you remembered.

And we whispered back: "Yes. That is it. Do that again."

Up Next

After empowering children to work consciously with energy, through intention, vibration, and play, we begin to see what they are truly capable of—but there is more. These children were not just born to remember. They were born to lead.

In the next chapter, we explore how today's telepathic, intuitive children are not just healers and dreamers, but the New Ancestors, anchoring the blueprint for a future we have only begun to imagine.

CHAPTER 14

The New Ancestors

These children are not ordinary; they are future ancestors in training.

They are not here to blend in.

They are not here to be "good."

They are here to shift timelines, rewrite family legacies, and remember out loud what humanity has tried to forget.

The children who walk among us now, telepathic, sensitive, empathic, emotionally intense, spiritually advanced beings, are not here to be shaped into the world. They are here to reshape the world itself.

They are what I call *The New Ancestors*.

In ancient traditions, ancestors were not just the ones behind us. They were also the ones who came back generation after generation, to continue their soul work. These children carry echoes of that knowing. Their eyes reflect lifetimes. Their presence bends time. And they are asking us for more than permission.

They are asking for partnership.

Who Are the New Ancestors?

The New Ancestors are children who:

1. Speak of past or parallel lives with clarity.
2. Feel emotion as frequency and truth as vibration.
3. React strongly to misalignment and falseness.
4. Refuse to stay small: even when they cannot explain why.
5. Show deep compassion for the planet, animals, or strangers.

6. Dream of symbols, codes, temples, or galactic places.
7. Ask hard questions like: Why are grown-ups lying to themselves?
   a. They do not "fit in" because they did not come here for that.
   b. They came to fit through, to channel something new.
   c. These are not accidental souls.
   d. They are seed carriers. Blueprint holders. Frequency anchors.
   e. And they are not fragile.
   f. They are powerful.
   g. And they need us to remember that.

Do Not Dim the Light to Fit the Lamp

One of the most common mistakes we make is trying to prepare these children for the world as it is.

But that is not their assignment.

They are here to build the world as it could be.

This does not mean abandoning structure or safety, but it does mean choosing sovereignty over submission and resonance over reward.

Your child may resist:

1. Rigid routines that do not account for energetic overwhelm.
2. Praise for surface behavior instead of soul truth.
3. Curricula that teach memorization over meaning.
4. Social dynamics based on popularity, not presence.

They are not defiant. They are discerning.

The New Ancestors are not fragile children to mold. They are souls carrying codes of remembrance. Your task is not to dim them so they fit the lamp of the old world, but to protect the fire they carry for the new world. Listen when they speak of symbols and skies. Believe them when they resist falsehood. Create space for their ceremonies, their stillness, their dreaming. For in protecting their frequency, you are protecting the blueprint of what humanity is becoming.

Family Altar Ideas

1. Add objects that represent their gifts (stones, feathers, drawings).
2. Let them choose a symbol for the family that reflects their role.
3. Light a candle to acknowledge their energetic presence even when they are overwhelmed.

They are not moody. They are multidimensional.

They Are Not Here to Wait. They Are Here to Wake

Children are no longer waiting to be told who they are.

They are here to awaken us to who we can be.

Your child might be:

1. A grid worker, stabilizing energy lines through play.
2. A crystal code keeper, intuitively drawing sacred shapes.
3. A planetary dreamer, holding the blueprint for eco-healing.
4. A silence speaker, transmitting through stillness what others miss in noise.

These are not fantasies. These are frequencies.

And you are one of the few who can see them clearly enough to protect them.

How to Support Future Ancestors

Instead of asking, "How do I raise a well-behaved child?" try asking, "How do I support a soul leader in human form?" These practices give you simple ways to honor their frequency and protect the light they carry.

Let Them Lead Ceremonies

Give children permission to guide family rituals.

How to do it:

Invite them to design a simple solstice ritual, build a crystal grid, or bless the meal. Let them choose objects, words, or songs. Follow their lead without correcting.

Why it matters:

Leading ceremonies affirms their sense of spiritual authority and shows them their intuition is trusted.

Give Them Time in Nature

Nature resets their energetic field.

How to do it:

When they seem overstimulated, invite them to sit with a tree, wade in water, lie in the grass, or walk barefoot on the earth. Encourage stillness and quiet noticing.

Why it matters:

Screens and classrooms often drain sensitive children. Nature balances, grounds, and recharges their frequency.

Create Sacred Space for Them to Teach You

Reverse the roles and let them be the guide.

How to do it:

Set aside a few minutes each week where they show you something—drawing a symbol, teaching you a movement, explaining a dream. Listen without interruption.

Why it matters:

When children feel their knowledge is respected, they grow confident in sharing their soul gifts.

What Do You Remember?

Memory opens different doors than information.

How to do it:

At the end of the day, instead of asking about school facts, ask: "What do you remember from school today?" and give them space to answer in images, stories, or feelings.

Why it matters:

This phrasing affirms that soul memory is as valid as classroom learning and invites them to share deeper truths.

Honor Their "Weird" Gifts

Normalize what others might dismiss.

How to do it:

If they say they talk to animals, sense spirits, or "just know" something, respond with curiosity rather than doubt. Ask: "Tell me more." Encourage them to journal or draw their experiences.

Why it matters:

Sensitive children often hide their gifts when they feel judged. By honoring their uniqueness, you keep their channels open.

Family Altar Ideas

A family altar becomes a living reminder that their energy matters.

How to do it:

Add objects that represent their gifts. Place stones, feathers, drawings, or meaningful tokens that reflect their interests.

Why it matters:

It validates that their contributions belong in the heart of the family.

Choose a Family Symbol

Invite your child to create or pick a symbol that represents your family.

How to do it:

Discuss symbols such as numbers, traffic signs, religious objects, etc. and how they can guide us for safety and convenience, or remind us of important things. You may expand this to team logos or mascots that create a special identity that sets it apart from others. Ask them to choose something and create an image on paper.

Why it matters:

This empowers them to define their role in the collective story.

Light a Candle for Their Presence

On hard days, when they feel overwhelmed, light a candle to honor their energy.

How to do it:

This toolbox has many related lessons. Begin this activity with a discussion of fire danger and fire safety and the use of matches. You can expand this to electrical outlets, plugs, stove tops, etc. by naming hot things. For older children you can discuss the triangle of heat, fuel and oxygen; fire stops burning when any one of these is used up or taken away.

You can continue by discussing the nature of liquid and solid. Explain how candle wax can change to liquid and back to solid. Ask what else can change from liquid to solid and back again.

You can discuss the effects candles can have on darkness in a room, how it can be seen from far away, and how it travels in all directions.

Why it matters:

The candle says: "You are still seen, even when you need space."

Science Note

Anthropologist Margaret Mead said, "Children must be taught how to think, not what to think."

Today's telepathic children do not need to be taught how to think: they need room to feel the field.

Dr. Bruce Lipton's work on epigenetics shows that environment shapes gene expression. When we nurture spiritual expression, telepathy, and intuition, we do not just preserve gifts; we activate them.

Dr. Daniel Siegel's concept of interpersonal neurobiology reminds us that nervous systems co-regulate; children raised in emotionally attuned, energetically aware homes are more likely to develop stronger intuition and resilience.

These are not "special kids." They are specially supported.

Practitioner Prompt

Ask yourself:

"What frequency does this child carry?"

"Which systems are dimming it?"

"How can I honor their leadership without burdening their path?"

Create a *Remembering Bundle* with the child:

- Include drawings, crystals, written intentions, or affirmations.
- Let the child choose a time capsule date to open it: 1 year, 5 years, or their future birthday.

This physical ritual helps anchor their memory of who they already are.

Telepathy Toolbox

These practices invite children to explore identity, memory, and leadership through play. Each one affirms that who they are goes beyond the present moment, connecting them to the deeper story of their soul.

The Name Before the Name

Discover identities beyond this lifetime.

How to do it:

1. Ask: *"If you had a name before this one, what was it?"*
2. Invite your child to draw or paint what that name feels like.
3. Emphasize that it does not have to be a "real" name—only one that resonates.

Why it works:

This helps children explore intuitive memory and symbolic self-expression, expanding their sense of identity beyond the current role.

Future Letter Channeling

Let their future self-speak into the present.

How to do it:

1. Invite your child to write a letter from their future self to their present self.
2. Ask them to include: *"What do I want you to remember?"*
3. Decorate and seal the letter.
4. Choose a future date to open it again.

Why it works:

Children learn to trust inner guidance as timeless. Channeling their future voice builds confidence and a sense of destiny.

Frequency Crown

Celebrate their unique leadership gift.

How to do it:

1. Create a crown together using crystals, foil, or colored paper.
2. Ask: *"What is your leadership gift?"* (e.g., kindness, courage, creativity).
3. Write the gift on the inside of the crown.
4. Let them wear it during family rituals or special moments.

Why it works:

The crown affirms their role as a leader in the family and honors their gifts as sacred.

Ancestral Mirror

See the deeper identities reflected within.

How to do it:

1. Sit quietly together with a mirror.
2. Ask your child to look into their own eyes and whisper: *"Who is in there?"*
3. Encourage them to write or draw who they see—animal, ancient, cosmic, or elemental.

Why it works:

Children often carry archetypal memories. This practice validates their multidimensional self-perception and gives them a safe way to express it.

Toolbox Wrap-Up

These activities remind children they are more than their current name, age, or role. By inviting them to meet their past, future, and symbolic selves, you open a doorway to ancestral memory and soul wisdom.

When children see their identity honored in this way, they no longer feel pressured to "fit in." Instead, they are empowered to carry their frequency proudly—as leaders, dreamers, and keepers of memory.

Invitation

You are not just raising a child.

You are raising a remembrance.

A living, breathing echo of what humanity used to know and what it must learn again.

Let your home be a place where Starseeds feel safe and let your language include their symbols.

Let your touch be an agreement, not a correction.

Let your silence be listening.

Let your parenting become partnership.

The world is shifting.

And your child did not just come to experience it.

They came to lead it.

We are already listening in color.

Dreaming in light.

Drawing codes into the dirt with our fingers.

We are not waiting for permission.

We are waiting for recognition.

When you remember who we are,

You remember who you are.

And when we walk together again,

The Earth will feel it.

Up Next

The book does not end here. The appendices have bonus material, tips and guidance to enrich your telepathic skills.

The real book has only just begun and it is flowing from the precious minds of your little ones. They are hoping and wanting to connect with you through your telepathic super-power.

Do not stop here. There is more in the following pages.

Stay soft.

Stay open.

Stay tuned.

And read on.

APPENDIX

APPENDIX A:

Glossary

Here is a concise reference to the key terms and concepts used throughout the book and answers to the most common questions from parents, educators, and caregivers who are new to working with intuitive or telepathic children.

Glossary of Terms

1. **Aura:**

   The subtle electromagnetic energy field that surrounds and interpenetrates the human body. Often perceived by sensitive individuals as color or sensation.

2. **Chakras:**

   Centers of energy in the subtle body that correspond to physical, emotional, and spiritual functions. Traditionally described as seven main spinning vortices along the spine, each with its own color and frequency.

3. **Clairaudience:**

   Clear hearing. The ability to perceive sounds, tones, or voices beyond the normal range.

4. **Clairalience:**

   Clear smelling. The ability to perceive scents that are not physically present (often linked to spiritual presence, memory, or energy).

5. **Claircognizance:**

   Clear knowing. Intuitive information that comes as sudden understanding or certainty without logical reasoning.

6. **Clairsentience:**

   Clear feeling. The ability to feel or sense the emotional or physical energy of others.

7. **Clairvoyance:**

   Clear seeing. The ability to perceive visual information, symbols, or scenes not visible to the physical eye.

8. **Coherence:**

   A state of harmony between the heart and brain, often associated with heightened intuition, peace, and empathy.

9. **Crystal Grids:**

   Arrangements of crystals placed in geometric patterns to focus energy, amplify intention, support healing, manifestation, and spiritual connection.

10. **Dowsing:**

    An intuitive technique that uses tools, (like pendulums or rods) to access subconscious knowledge or energetic information.

11. **Energy Field:**

    The vibrational, non-physical aspect of a living being that interacts with the surrounding environment; sometimes called the *biofield*.

12. **Energy Vampire:**

    A person or situation that unconsciously drains life force energy from others, often leaving others feeling depleted or fatigued.

13. **Etheric Body:**

    The subtle energy body closest to the physical body, serving as a bridge between the physical and spiritual realms. It reflects health, vitality, and imbalances.

14. **Frequency:**

The rate at which energy vibrates. Different emotions, thoughts, and states of being carry different frequencies or vibrations.

15. **Grounding:**

The practice of connecting one's energy to the Earth to restore balance, stability, and presence in the physical body. Techniques include walking barefoot, visualizations, or working with nature.

16. **Heart-Brain Coherence:**

A physiological and energetic state where the rhythms of the heart, brain, and nervous system are synchronized.

17. **Light Language:**

A nonverbal, energetic form of communication using sound, tone, symbol, or movement that bypasses the rational mind and connects soul-to-soul.

18. **Morphic Resonance:**

A theory that behavior and memory can be transmitted across space and time through fields shared by similar forms.

19. **Nonlocal Communication:**

The ability to send or receive information without the use of physical senses, often referred to as telepathy.

20. **Pineal Gland:**

A small gland in the brain associated with intuition, sleep cycles, and spiritual insight; often called the third eye.

21. **Telepathy:**

The transmission of thoughts, emotions, or information directly from one mind to another without verbal or sensory cues.

22. **Theta Brainwaves:**

A brainwave state associated with deep relaxation, imagination, and early childhood development. It allows greater access to the subconscious.

APPENDIX B:

Frequently Asked Questions

1. Do all children have telepathic abilities?

Yes. Every child is born with natural intuitive and energetic awareness. Telepathy is part of our original wiring, but it often fades when dismissed or ignored.

2. Is telepathy real?

Yes. Both ancient traditions and modern research suggest telepathy is a natural human capacity. Studies in neuroscience, quantum biology, and energy medicine show that thought and emotion can travel beyond the brain as measurable energy.

3. What if I do not feel intuitive myself?

To be telepathic and better able to support your child, you do not have to be psychic. This book helps adults reconnect with their natural, intuitive senses through simple, everyday practices and activities.

4. How can I support my telepathic child?

Trust is the foundation. Create safe spaces for your child to share what they see, feel, or hear. Encourage them with playful activities like silent communication or dream journaling. Most importantly, listen with an open heart.

5. Will my child lose telepathy as they grow older?

Not necessarily. Children's natural telepathy may fade if ignored, denied, or ridiculed. However, when supported, practiced, and honored, it can strengthen into adulthood.

6. Will using these tools conflict with my spiritual or religious beliefs?

No. Telepathy is based on universal principles of connection, love, and presence. It is so natural that many animals use it.

7. Can these practices help in traditional school settings?

Absolutely. Many activities, such as coherence breathing, silent communication, and emotion tracking, can enhance focus, reduce anxiety, and improve empathy in classrooms.

8. Do I need special training to use this book?

No. The Telepathy Toolbox games and practices are designed to be accessible, intuitive, and fun. Whether you are a parent, educator, or healer, you can begin today.

9. What if my child does not respond to the activities?

Be patient and playful. Every child opens in their own way. Sometimes, they respond later in dreams or conversations. Keep the energy light and trust the process.

10. What about skeptics?

Skepticism is natural. You do not have to convince anyone. Simply honor your child's experience. Truth does not always need agreement to be real.

11. How can I balance trusting my child and trusting myself?

Trust is about balance. Believe your child's experiences while also honoring your own inner wisdom. When you listen to both, you create safety, respect, and guidance for your child to grow.

12. Can siblings or friends practice telepathy together?

Yes. Children often find it easier to practice with peers or siblings because play reduces self-consciousness. Shared activities strengthen both connection and skill.

13. What if my child shares something that feels frightening?

Stay calm, listen, and reassure them. Children sometimes pick up on emotions, dreams, or energies they do not yet understand. Encourage them to describe what they feel, then help them ground, breathe, and release fear.

14. Can telepathy be confused with imagination?

At times, yes. Imagination and telepathy both use the inner senses. Rather than dismissing an experience, treat it as valid. With practice, children learn to distinguish between creative play and genuine energetic communication.

15. Is telepathy safe?

Yes, when practiced with healthy boundaries. Like any form of communication, it is important to teach children to say yes or no, to rest when tired, and to shield or ground if they feel overwhelmed.

16. How does grounding help telepathic children?

Grounding connects a child's energy to the Earth, providing balance and stability. It helps prevent overwhelm and keeps intuitive experiences integrated with everyday life.

17. Can telepathic skills help with emotional regulation?

Absolutely. Practices such as coherence breathing, silent listening, and energy awareness teach children how to recognize emotions early, calm their system, and respond rather than react.

18. What if my child stops talking about their experiences?

Do not assume the ability is gone. Sometimes children go quiet if they sense disbelief or lack of interest. Keep creating safe, welcoming spaces, and the sharing often returns.

19. Do adults regain telepathic abilities too?

Yes. Many adults find that as they detox their environment, quiet the mind, and practice simple techniques, their own telepathic senses return. This book is for adults as much as it is for children.

Remember: telepathy is not about perfection but presence. Trust your child's subtle experiences, and trust your own ability to hold space. Mutual trust strengthens the bond and opens the channel for clearer communication.

20. Is it safe for a Christian to be telepathic?

Yes. Telepathy is a spiritual gift that comes with being human. Scripture shows God can reveal hidden things (*Matt. 9:4; 2 Kgs. 6:12*), so the capacity itself is not the issue; how we use it is. It is the action and intention that matters, not the channel. Does it lead to peace, humility, and love (*Gal. 5:22-23*), or fear, pride, and isolation?

If you have any concerns, hearing others' thoughts or having intrusive experiences that distress you, it is wise to talk with a qualified mental-health professional or a pastor.

APPENDIX C:

Science and Sources

This appendix summarizes the key scientific voices, concepts, and findings referenced throughout the book. These pioneers help validate intuitive and telepathic awareness with biological, neurological, and quantum insight.

Dean Radin, Ph.D. – Chief Scientist, *Institute of Noetic Sciences* (IONS)

Key Contribution:
Radin has conducted decades of peer-reviewed research into telepathy, intuition, and nonlocal perception. His Ganzfeld experiments showed statistically significant results for image transfer across distance, while his presentiment studies demonstrated that the human body responds seconds before emotional events occur. He is also author of *Entangled Minds* and *The Conscious Universe*.

Relevance:
His work offers empirical validation for telepathic knowing, supporting the idea that children's intuitive abilities are measurable and scientifically grounded.

Stephen Porges, Ph.D. – Neuroscientist, Developer of the *Polyvagal Theory*

Key Contribution:

Porges' *Polyvagal Theory* demonstrates that the human nervous system is wired for connection and safety long before language develops. His work highlights the role of the Vagus nerve in regulating emotional resonance, social engagement, and nonverbal attunement.

Relevance:

Provides the biological foundation for understanding why sensitive children are so deeply tuned to nonverbal fields of communication.

Stuart Brown, M.D. – Founder, *National Institute for Play*

Key Contribution:

Brown's research shows that play is a *biological necessity*, shaping brain development, social bonding, creativity, and trust.

Relevance:

Validates why playful telepathic practices are so effective in rebuilding trust and connection between parent and child.

Lev Vygotsky – Developmental Psychologist

Key Contribution:

Vygotsky introduced the concept of the *zone of proximal development*, emphasizing how play allows children to stretch beyond their current capacities in a safe, imaginative space.

Relevance:

Supports the use of symbolic games and imagination as natural training grounds for telepathic communication.

Jean Piaget, Ph.D. – Developmental Psychologist

Key Contribution:

Piaget studied how children construct knowledge through active exploration. He called play *the work of childhood*, showing how children test, build, and solidify understanding through creative interaction.

Relevance:

Reinforces the idea that telepathic games are not trivial, but fundamental learning experiences.

Researchers and Scientific Contributors

Veda Austin

Field: Water consciousness research

Key Insight: Demonstrated that water responds to human intention and emotion. Her photographic method shows that water can *hear* words, music, and thoughts, forming crystal-like imagery that reflects communication.

Referenced in: Chapter 4

Website: vedaustin.com

Cleve Backster

Field: Polygraph science, plant consciousness

Key Insight: Demonstrated that plants, brine shrimp, and even yogurt cultures respond to human thoughts and emotions. His experiments suggested that telepathy and bio-communication exist beyond human language.

Referenced in: Chapter 4

Website: There does not seem to be an official website.

Gregg Braden – *Divine Matrix*

Field: Spiritual science, metaphysics

Key Insight: A unifying field connects all things. Children's *knowing* comes from direct access to this matrix of consciousness.

Referenced in: Chapter 12
Website: greggbraden.com

Lee Carroll—"KRYON" Channel

Field: Channeling / consciousness & metaphysics. Wikipedia

Key Insight: Teaches that humanity is in a long-term shift in consciousness; emphasizes activating the body's Innate intelligence for self-healing and accessing the Akash, and introduces esoteric models like the "12 Layers of DNA." Early KRYON messages spoke of the Earth's "magnetic service."

Referenced in: Endorsements, Chapter 8 and Appendix F
Website: Kryon.com

Dr. Rosalind Franklin

Field: Biophysics, molecular biology

Key Insight: Discovered DNA's double-helix structure through X-ray crystallography. Her legacy supports that energy, light, and pattern are encoded in cellular memory.

Referenced in: Chapters 6, 8
Website: rosalindfranklinsociety.org/rosalind-franklin

Jonathan & Andi Goldman

Field: Sound healing, vibrational medicine

Key Insight: Sound and humming create measurable shifts in coherence, heart–brain synchronization, and the human energy field, supporting nonlocal connection and intuitive communication.

Referenced in: Chapter 3
Website: healingsounds.com

HeartMath Institute

Field: Psychophysiology, coherence science

Key Insight: The electromagnetic field of the heart can synchronize with others, improving emotional connection and intuitive accuracy.

Referenced in: Chapters 1, 3, 5, 6, 7, 9, and 10
Website: HeartMath.org

Dr. Bruce Lipton – *Biology of Belief: Unleashing the Power of Consciousness, Matter, and Miracles*

Field: Epigenetics, developmental biology

Key Insight: Our thoughts, stemming from our beliefs and perceptions, shape our biology. Our complex mind generates the chemical and emotional signals that direct cell behavior.

Referenced in: Chapters 1, 2, 11
Website: brucelipton.com

Lynne McTaggart – *The Field*

Field: Science journalism, consciousness studies

Key Insight: Thoughts and intentions can affect matter across distance. Her research explores a quantum field connecting all life.

Referenced in: Chapters 8, 11, 12
Website: lynnemctaggart.com

Dr. Bradley Nelson

Author of *The Body Code® / The Emotion Code® / The Heart Code® / The Belief Code®*

Field: Energy medicine, subconscious healing

Key Insight: Emotional baggage and limiting beliefs can block intuition and health. His system helps clear those blocks for better clarity and energy flow.

Referenced in: Endorsements, Forward, and Chapter 11
Website: discoverhealing.com

Dr. Candace Pert – *Molecules of Emotion*

Field: Neuroscience, psychopharmacology

Key Insight: Emotions are biochemical messengers affecting every cell in the body. They bridge mind and body—and may carry intuitive data.

Referenced in: Chapters 2, 6
Website: candacepert.com

Dr. Beverly Rubik

Field: Biophysics, consciousness studies

Key Insight: The human biofield, a scientifically measurable energy field, plays a role in health, healing, and subtle energetic communication.

Referenced in: Chapter 6
Website: beverlyrubik.com

Rupert Sheldrake, Ph.D. – *Morphic Resonance Theory*

Field: Developmental biology, parapsychology

Key Insight: Memory and behavior may be transmitted through morphic fields: a nonlocal system of energetic patterning.

Referenced in: Chapters 3, 5, 7
Website: sheldrake.org

Dr. Daniel Siegel – *Interpersonal Neurobiology*

Field: Neuroscience, child psychology

Key Insight: The brain is shaped through relational resonance. Mirror neurons allow for emotional attunement, especially between caregivers and children.

Referenced in: Chapters 3, 5, 7, 9
Website: drdansiegel.com

Susan V. Whittaker,

Author of *The Complete Guide to Crystal Therapy: For the Body, Mind, and Spirit – Volumes 1 and 2*

Field: Crystal therapy, energy medicine

Key Insight: Crystals can be programmed with intention and used to restore energetic harmony. The-book includes 2,700 dowsing charts for 1,111 different crystals.

Referenced in: Chapter 13
Website: DeTOXalot.com

Author of *Diving Deep Into the Ocean of The Mind: A Dowser's Guide for Exploring, Empowering, and Elevating Your Energy Using Your Subconscious Mind*

Field: Soul development

Key Insight: The book's 535 pendulum dowsing charts use drill-down logic to select from several thousand topics a guiding phrase that is in one's highest and best good. It facilitates seeking beyond knowledge with curiosity and trust and help from outside the mind.

Referenced in: Chapter 13
Website: DeTOXalot.com

Author of *Broad Spectrum DeTOX* – **Frequency-Based Detoxification**

Field: Quantum detox, vibrational medicine

Key Insight: Developed by Dr. Susan V. Whittaker, Broad Spectrum DeTOX uses frequency imprints embedded in non-consumable bottles of sand, copper, and crystals to support the body's ability to regulate and self-heal. The system addresses twelve categories of toxins, including heavy metals, chemicals, nanoparticles, EMFs, vaccines, and emotional residues and invasive life forms.

In a 30-month study, participants demonstrated strategic detoxification across all categories without harsh purging effects.

Referenced in: Chapters 11, 13 and Appendix H
Website: DeTOXalot.com

Inventor of *Clearest Benefits Program* – **EMF and Energetic Shielding**

Field: Subtle energy shielding, EMF protection

Key Insight: Developed by Dr. Whittaker, the *Clearest Benefits Program* provides scheduled energetic clearing and shielding to reduce the impact of electromagnetic fields and environmental stressors.

The program targets disruptive influences such as dirty electricity, 5G, Wi-Fi, smart meters, emotional interference, spiritual attachments, and geopathic stress. Independent assessments and participant reports note improvements in clarity, resilience, and overall energetic balance.

Referenced in: Appendix F
Website: AClearBenefit.com

Additional Scientific Concepts

Theta Brainwave States

Insight: Children under age seven, spend most of their time in theta brainwave states which is ideal for subconscious programming and nonverbal reception.

Referenced in: Chapters 1, 2

Nonlocal Consciousness / Quantum Biology

Insight: Thought, emotion, and awareness may not be limited to time and space. Modern quantum theory supports intuitive perception and subtle energy transfer.

Referenced in: Chapters 3, 9

Primary Sources on Reincarnation and Children's Memories

Referenced in: Chapter 12
- Dr. Ian Stevenson: documented cases
- James Leininger: child memories
- Shanti Devi: case study
- Vishwa Nath: case study
- Savitri Devi Pathak: case study

Primary Source: Translations of Sumerian Tablets (e.g., *The Epic of Atrahasis*)

Together, these sources show the convergence of science and spirituality. The more we listen to the wisdom of the body and the research of these pioneers, the more we see: telepathy is not fantasy, but a forgotten faculty now being remembered.

Quick Start Guide
for Parents, Teachers, Families and Caregivers

Welcome. You hold more than a book—it is a treasure map that helps you stay connected, or become connected, to the deepest bonds humans can share. What was nearly lost in the noise of modern life is still present—waiting for anyone willing to pause, remember, and help others remember too.

This remembering is profoundly important for families and future generations. The natural love that grows perceptibly within a woman—and becomes visible in families of every kind—never disappears. It may be suppressed or forgotten, but it cannot be extinguished. It is universal and deeper than we can imagine.

The activities in this book have no boundaries and no limits on their capacity for success. They came from an unbroken string of shamans and elders who had little contact with "the world" as we know it. They planted sacred seeds in the author's heart foreseeing her path, the changes ahead and the need for this book. This is no small gift. The book is filled with tips, tools, games and learning activities. These are essential tools for the survival of humanity in the journey ahead.

These sacred leaders have now passed on. They were chosen channels for passing on ancient wisdom and the intuitive power of relational communication and lifelong bonding. They have profoundly achieved their mission through the pages of this book by creating waves of ancient wisdom and human skills to help countless future generations, as their forefathers did for them. The mission is now in your hands, too.

Follow the Process

The book is to be read in the order given. Each chapter opens a layer of remembering, insight, and activation. This is not a recommendation but an instruction from the guides behind the creation of this book for optimizing your progress and its rewards. Here is guidance on how to get the most from the recurring symbols:

Telepathy Toolbox

Look for this text to find play-based practices and games you can do with children. These help to build nonverbal communication, energetic sensitivity, and connection--perfect for home, classroom, or therapy.

Great for: Parents, teachers, homeschoolers, caregivers.

Practitioner Prompt

These notes are written for caregivers, therapists, and educators. They encourage deeper reflection and may include ways to apply ideas in client or group settings.

Great for: Counselors, energy workers, coaches, advanced readers.

Science Note

This text marks evidence-based validation of intuitive phenomena, including insights from quantum biology, neuropsychology, HeartMath Institute, and more.

Great for: Skeptical readers, science lovers, researchers, and clinicians looking for grounding.

Invitation

These sections distill each chapter into a final energetic call. They often restate the deepest truths in simple language--perfect for closing reflections or journal prompts.

Great for: Everyone. Especially helpful when you're short on time and need a meaningful takeaway.

Transmission from the Telepathic Ones

These messages are not instructions. They are reminders. Each one is a brief channeled message offered from the intuitive realms to help you remember what has always been within you. These passages speak directly to your field, not your ears, awakening the natural telepathic awareness you and your child were born with.

Read them slowly. Let them settle.

They are designed to gently realign your inner sensing, deepen family connection, and open the doorway to clearer intuition. Through these messages, you are reminded that guidance is always available, and that you and your child are already part of a larger conversation of energy, presence, and knowing.

Daily & Weekly Use Ideas

Just one tool per day or week can shift a child's perception--and yours.

- **Choose a Toolbox game** from any chapter and play it together.
- **Pick a Practitioner Prompt** to reflect on before a session or school day.
- **Revisit one Science Note** and share it with someone curious but unsure.
- **Use a Final Invitation** as a journal prompt or circle discussion theme.
- **Read a Transmission aloud** at the end of a homeschool week or family dinner.

Final Reminder

You do not need permission to trust what you feel. You only need practice.

They practice activities will guide you, one symbol, one game, one frequency at a time, back to the language you never truly lost.

APPENDIX E
Vibrational Curriculum Sampler

A Glimpse into the Telepathic Schools of the Future

Subject	Example Activity	Purpose
Vibrational Geometry	Chladni Plate & Sand	Show how sound shapes matter and organizes energy.
Emotional Frequencies	Tone + Color Mapping	Teach children how emotions feel and appear energetically.
Quantum Arts	Spoon Bending	Practice focused intention and mind-over-matter skills.
Telepathic Communication	Silent Thought Circles	Strengthen nonverbal communication and empathy.
Energy Technology	Build Crystal Grids	Explore how intention, shape, and stone combine to transmit energy.

Subject	Example Activity	Purpose
Group Coherence	Heart-Brain Synchronization Breathing	Develop unity, calm, and intuitive accuracy.
Etheric Architecture	Design Sacred Space with Light Codes	Learn how energy and intention create invisible structures.
Remote Viewing	View Hidden Objects Using Coordinates	Activate nonlocal perception and subtle data retrieval.
Clairvoyant Visualization	Symbol Interpretation Games	Build intuitive visual literacy.
Earth Wisdom	Communicate with Trees or Plants	Tune into nature's consciousness and subtle responses.
Emotional Literacy	Project Emotions as Color + Light	Cultivate emotional awareness and expression through frequency.
Elemental Alchemy	Practice Balancing Earth, Air, Fire, Water, Ether	Understand elemental energies within self and world.
Energetic Healing	Hands-on Aura Soothing	Empower children to balance energy fields naturally.

APPENDIX F:

Index: Telepathy Toolboxes and the Games

Because parents will often want to revisit an activity quickly, there are two lists in this appendix. One is like a table of contents for each chapter. The other is an alphabetical list that shows the chapter where the activities can be found.

The telepathy toolboxes and games are the heart of the book's practicality. They are simple, playful practices that make telepathy and intuitive connection something families and practitioners can experience and refine every day. Most of them can be used in one-on-one settings or adapted for small gatherings with participants of any age. Let the lists serve you as seeds for discovery

This appendix is not meant to replace the depth and context found in the chapters themselves, but to serve as a quick guide when you want to bring a new game, ritual, or practice into daily life.

The lists serve as a reminder that you do not have to go quickly or do things in any given order. Choose practices that feel natural, keep them lighthearted, and let them grow into a family rhythm over time.

Chapter List

Chapter 1 – Born Knowing: The Telepathic Infant
- Heart-Listening Telepathy
- The Quiet Heart Game
- Feel-What-I-Feel Game
- Telepathy & Body Language Matching Game
- Sibling Connection Game
- Lightbulb Images
- Silent Soothing
- Sibling Soul Talk
- Dream Sharing
- Pre-Verbal Check-In
- Emotion Echo Cards

Chapter 2 – Thought Before Language
- Mirror Me with No Words
- Feel My Field
- Color the Feeling

Chapter 3 – Energy Fields and Morphic Resonance
- Feel It First
- Sound and Soothe
- Symbol Basket
- Image Sharing
- Dreamtime Drawing
- Tone Tracking

Chapter 4 – How We Shut It Down
- Draw the Dream That Did Not Get Shared
- What Was Not Said
- The Unseen Friend Game
- Float the Feeling
- The Listening Candle

Chapter 5 – Signs Your Child is Using Telepathy

- Eye-to-Eye Images
- Silent Guessing Games
- Drawing Each Other's Thoughts
- Bedtime Messages
- Family Telepathy Play
- Honoring Insights

Chapter 6 – Autism, Silence, and the Secret Language

- Vibration Drawing
- Silent Matching Game
- Tone Together
- Symbol Show-and-Tell
- Star Blanket Time

Chapter 7 – Rebuilding Telepathic Trust with Your Child

- Image Sharing Game
- Story Snapshots
- Picture Ping-Pong
- Heart Coherence Breathing
- Heartbeat Match
- Heart Whisper
- Mutual Silence and Mirroring
- Mirror Me Play
- Thought Transmission Practice
- Guess the Number
- Telepathic Charades
- Emotion Radar
- Deck of Intuition
- One Minute of Shared Stillness
- Tuning Into the Emotional Field
- Sound Ping
- Feel and Draw
- Journaling and Dream Sharing
- Telepathy Journal

- Telepathic Story Stones
- Light Signature Drawing
- Message from the Trees

Chapter 11 – Remembering What You Never Lost

- Symbol Tuning
- Tree Whispering
- Frequency Anchoring

Chapter 12 – Soul Memory and the Ones Who Remember

- Soul Memory Match
- Star Map Drawing
- Past Life Echo Objects
- Portal Walk
- Who Am I Today?

Chapter 13 – Programming the Invisible

- Turn crystals into helpers and companions.
- Water
- Stones or Shells
- Drawings & Mandalas
- Color Codes
- Morning Light Programming
- Bedtime Beam
- Lunchtime Charging
- Hand Activation
- Thoughtform Toss
- Programmed Ice
- Glow Stone Activation
- Intention Jars
- Crystal Charging Circle
- Feel the Room Game

Chapter 14 – The New Ancestors

- Let Them Lead Ceremonies
- Give Them Time in Nature

Alphabetical List

APPENDIX G:

Children Still See the Other Side

(KRYON, publicly channeled by Lee Carroll, 10/12/25)

"… Did you know that children, as they grow up, the first thing they are aware of is that they are not alone. I do not mean the parents are hovering, I mean that there are other kinds of things in their room with them. Have you ever seen an infant and you buy them some kind of fancy mobile thing that moves around and has lights and makes sounds? The infant then looks over there in the corner of the room instead? It goes ha-ha-ha. And you say, look at what I got you, not over there. There's nothing over there. And the child; they know better. They are looking at a swirling ball of light over there that you cannot see. They are seeing the esoterics. In the first few months of their life, dear ones, they are still on the other side—in some ways. They still have 5th dimensional views of things—in some ways. They are attracted many times by things you cannot see. And by energies you are not aware of.

"How many of you lightworkers will walk into a room or a space or perhaps you are in an airport and there's a very small infant? And because you are there that infant will turn its head and look at you and smile. Because you are broadcasting light that is multidimensional and that infant knows it. Then you lose it. Or, you are talked out of it by your parents "de-facto-ly."

"It is time to get real. It is time to rekindle that—all of you. I want you to go backwards and think about it: what was it, perhaps, that I had? That is the beauty of full-time communication with the creative source of the universe. It is in your DNA…

217

"…You were born magnificent like that beautiful little baby who could still see the other side of the veil. And you still are there."

KRYON's message highlights the reality of telepathy and the rewards for adults who rekindle their own abilities. He reminds us that infants are still "on the other side in some ways," perceiving light, energy, and presence that adults often overlook. KRYON's message about telepathy not only affirms what this book describes, but was channeled to an audience where the author sat only a few feet from Lee Carroll. Lee Carroll had not met or talked with the author and had no possible way of knowing a near final draft of this book was with her.

Perhaps, KRYON knew she had traveled to Colorado to learn about Lee Carroll and was sitting nearby during this transmission. And, perhaps, the morning when the author woke up with this whole book in her mind and a sense of urgency to write it, it was KRYON who had asked and commissioned her to get this message sent out.

Author's Note

The reflections in this book about infants who still "see the other side" were written months before the KRYON channeling was released. When I later heard KRYON speak these same words, it felt like a loving confirmation from the field—that truth often arrives through more than one messenger. I extend my heartfelt gratitude to Lee Carroll, the voice of KRYON, for his lifetime of work reminding humanity of its divine potential and for so beautifully affirming the message of this book.

When Telepathy Seems Lost

The Nervous System's Role in Telepathic Communication

1. Telepathy and the Developing Nervous System

Telepathy, intuition, and empathic perception are natural abilities, especially in early childhood. Before spoken language becomes dominant, children communicate energetically, emotionally, and intuitively. They sense intention and emotional tone long before they rely on words.

As children grow, speech gradually becomes the primary channel. Telepathy does not disappear; attention simply shifts away from it. The intuitive capacity remains within every child—and every adult. It is part of how the human nervous system receives and sends information.

The nervous system is the bridge between the physical world and the intuitive world. When obstructions such as neurotoxins, chronic infections, or other invasive organisms are reduced, this bridge clears and subtle communication becomes easier to experience. A balanced nervous system is open, receptive, and able to process delicate signals. An imbalanced one—overloaded or stressed—may struggle to receive or interpret intuitive communication.

2. How Neurotoxins Influence Telepathic Sensitivity

Modern life exposes children and adults to environmental neurotoxins from the very start. Studies examining umbilical cord blood have identified more than 280 industrial chemicals and neurotoxic compounds present before birth. This means many children begin life already carrying a measurable burden.

Because this is so prevalent, a child who seems to show little or no telepathic ability may be experiencing nutritional gaps or a systemic imbalance—not a lack of ability. In some cases, these imbalances can be greatly improved with appropriate support.

Where there are signs of impaired nervous system development, the situation deserves closer attention. In some cases, this may indicate that a system or function needs help performing its natural detoxification and regulatory roles. Concerns about learning difficulties or behavioral irregularities may be referred to practitioners with a history of success or qualified medical professionals.

There are reports of telepathic-type experiences increasing under certain conditions. Some researchers and practitioners are interested in exploring the possible biological and energetic mechanisms behind such cases. Because the nervous system is the bridge between the physical and intuitive worlds, a balanced system makes it easier for children to notice, trust, and use their natural telepathic awareness.

Neurotoxin-related imbalance can influence:
- emotional steadiness
- sensory processing
- learning and integration
- subtle intuitive signals
- telepathic communication

It's Not Your Fault

Many parents—especially mothers—quietly worry they did something wrong when a child struggles with sensitivity or telepathy. But modern environmental exposures are unintentional and unavoidable. These toxins are present virtually everywhere including in the air, water, food, and home environments.

The Environmental Working Group (EWG), a non-profit consumer health advocacy organization surveyed 2,300 women in the U.S. to study their personal care product use. They found that the average woman uses products containing 168 different chemicals before breakfast.

There is very little public education and a lot of corporate policies that are not intended to make people healthy. What matters most is education, understanding, and support.

3. A Balanced Nervous System Supports Natural Telepathy

Children flourish when their nervous systems are balanced and responsive. A balanced system helps them:

- regulate emotions
- notice subtle impressions
- integrate sensory experiences
- remain calm and connected
- communicate intuitively with caregivers

Just as a steady environment makes it easier to hear quiet sounds, a balanced nervous system makes telepathic perception more natural and accessible.

Where balance exists, intuitive connection deepens.

4. Reawakening Telepathy in Adults

Adults do not lose telepathy with age—they lose conscious access to it when spoken language becomes dominant around seven years old. The activities in this book help adults reconnect with the intuitive pathways that were active long before reliance on speech.

This remembering process becomes smoother when the nervous system is supported physically. Decades of exposure can create a quiet, cumulative burden that disrupts balance and makes subtle perception more effortful. Reducing this burden does not create telepathy; it simply removes what unsettles it.

If remembering feels unusually slow or difficult, it may be a sign that the body would benefit from additional support, including a comprehensive detoxification program. Some whole-body energetic systems—such as Broad Spectrum DeTOX program—offer assessments and support that can be provided without office visits.

5. Telepathic Families and Deep Bonds

Telepathy does not arise in isolation—it thrives in the relational spaces between people. Families who share strong emotional safety, trust, and affection often experience intuitive communication as a natural part of daily life. Telepathic families commonly observe:

- intuitive awareness and bonding between siblings
- instant emotional understanding
- silent knowing between parents and children
- deeper, more joyful connection

Telepathy strengthens the "family field," allowing relationships and communication to flourish in the family. Because it is a subtle energy that flourishes in clean, balanced nervous systems, early education about good food and environmental hazards is an important subject to revisit often.

As children grow up and become parents themselves, these loving, telepathic bonds can become an on-going family legacy.

6. A Waning Sense of Connectedness

The sense of connectedness is an effect of the innate intuitive capacities used naturally in childhood before spoken language took center stage. Connectedness itself does not disappear with age; the underlying intuitive capacity remains. However, if the sense of connectedness seems to fade, it is often because something is disturbing the nervous system—such as environmental toxins, chronic stress, or unresolved emotional pain.

This is not an age based problem. Its symptoms can show up at any time and even start in the womb.

Children with Neurotoxin Burdens

When children carry high levels of neurotoxins, their social, emotional, physical and mental development can be noticeably impacted:

- learning delays

- attention difficulties
- reduced performance
- slower cognitive processing
- emotional dysregulation
- sensory overload
- difficulty keeping up with normal maturation
- reduced intuitive or telepathic clarity

These children are not "behind" in everything. They are burdened—but often gifted in many ways. Their system has too much interference, while their natural brilliance is still trying to shine through the fog.

---

7. Invitation for Families Seeking More Information

This book was written to help children retain their natural telepathic abilities and to help adults remember their own. If you feel that neurological interference, environmental exposure, or developmental challenges may be affecting your or your child's intuitive abilities, or your own, you are welcome to reach out for more information.

For details about assessments, support programs, or how this system may help enhance balance and intuitive communication within your family, please contact:

Sue Whittaker
Email: Sue@DeTOXalot.com
Website: DeTOXalot.com

Navigating Through the Awakening

Telepathic connection within a family is one of the most beautiful experiences a person can have. As you and your child remember skills you never truly lost, you may want to share your journey with friends, extended family, teachers, or your community.

Not everyone will be immediately open or enthusiastic. Some may not understand, some may feel uncertain, and others may have concerns shaped by their upbringing, beliefs, or cultural stories. This appendix offers gentle, grounded responses to the kinds of questions, objections, or misunderstandings you may encounter as you support your child through this magical stage of development.

Mini Table of Contents

Before We Begin, Let's Look at What Telepathy Is *Not*

A great deal of confusion comes from books, movies, TV shows and myths. So, it helps to be clear about what telepathy does not involve.

Telepathy is not:

- mind reading
- scanning someone's thoughts
- uncovering secrets
- eavesdropping on another person's inner world
- mental manipulation
- forcing someone to think or feel something
- bypassing another person's free will

Telepathy is more like:

- sensing feelings
- perceiving impressions
- deep listening
- relational intuition
- emotional resonance
- heart-to-heart awareness

A simple way to express this to others is:

> *"Telepathy is more like emotional resonance than reading someone's private thoughts."*

This description may help others regard telepathy as a natural extension of empathy, not a supernatural intrusion.

A Foundation of Respect and Sovereignty

Telepathy is never about invading privacy or taking control. It is not mentalism, hypnosis, influence, or any form of power over another person's will. True telepathic connection is relational, respectful, and always rooted in personal sovereignty—a deep understanding that every person has a sacred right to their own mind, inner life, and boundaries.

You may want to help your child understand that telepathy cannot "tap into" someone who does not want connection. It appears only where there is mutual attunement and trust, much like sensing a loved one's mood when they walk into a room.

In this way, telepathy is not an extraordinary "power," but a heightened awareness that honors the autonomy of every individual. When practiced with kindness and charity, it becomes a beautiful extension of the love that already exists within your family.

---

1. Anchoring Parents in Love and Responsibility

Research in epigenetics, popularized by authors such as Bruce Lipton, suggests that a mother's inner environment—her stress or her peace, her fear or her joy—can influence how a child's biology expresses itself. That culture becomes the womb that holds not just their body, but their soul. Even in the prenatal stage, the child is listening, absorbing, and attuning. Every vibration of joy, every moment of stress, every word spoken with tenderness or fear is shaping their field of awareness.

Science now confirms what many parents have intuited: a child absorbs not only emotional fields but also chemical ones. Research in epigenetics, such as the work of Bruce Lipton, shows that a mother's inner environment—her stress or her peace, her fear or her joy—literally shapes the baby's biology. A mother in prolonged stress may send chemical signals that prepare a child to be a fighter, quick to survive. A mother who feels safe and supported passes on signals that prepare a child to trust, bond, and thrive.

The prenatal world is the child's first classroom—a blend of biochemical and telepathic messages about life outside the womb. This environment profoundly influences the development of virtually every aspect of the child. Even details we often think of as fixed, such as the clarity and brightness of the eyes, can be shaped by the mother's nutrition and lifestyle.

This means parents are not simply caretakers who "begin the job" at birth. They are the first and ongoing architects of the child's inner world. And this responsibility does not expire. From the womb onward, the child continues to draw from the parent's presence, love, and protection—telepathically sensing whether the foundation is secure.

Here is the great reassurance: parents do not need to be perfect. Children do not telepathically record perfection—they record love. Love is the strongest signal, the most powerful field. It covers faults, heals mistakes, and provides a constant anchor, even in the chaos of everyday life.

And because children feel their parents 'love telepathically, perfection is unnecessary. What the child needs most is the felt sense of being cherished, protected, validated—and cared for. Not every child arrives into circumstances that feel fully welcoming. At times, a child may sense hesitation, fear, or tension around their arrival. But this does not need to define them. Through intentional telepathic connection, the parent's field of love can evolve and grow more positive, sending the ongoing message: "You are loved, you are safe, you belong."

In a world where teachers, pastors, and experts, sometimes act as if they know better than parents, it is easy to lose confidence. But no one knows or loves a child as a parent does. This is not rebellion against authority; it is the fulfillment of a responsibility that has existed for millennia—to hold the life of the child as sacred, to guide their path with love, and to remain their anchor no matter what culture or belief system says.

Children feel this. They know—not just intellectually, but telepathically—whether their parent is standing firm in love and protection. That anchoring is their greatest safety, their greatest security, and their greatest joy.

This section exists to validate and empower parents as they navigate people, culture, and belief systems that may misunderstand or discourage telepathy. With practical tools and guiding principles, you can stand firm in your role as protector and guide. You do not need to be flawless to be enough. What matters is the constancy of your love—the one signal your child will always recognize.

2. When Others Push Back

Sharing your joy with your child's telepathic journey is natural. But not everyone you meet will celebrate it. Some will be curious, others cautious, and some may dismiss it outright. Teachers, pastors, relatives, and even professionals may speak as if they know more about your child than you do.

This can feel discouraging or even demeaning, but remember, their opinions do not outweigh your connection. Parental responsibility is rooted in love. This is known, seen and felt by your child. Some cultures may believe the schools, the government, the multi-generational family or the village has a role of responsibility above the parents. Those situations are complex and may have aspects you agree with and some you don't. Let love be your guide.

Pushback Voices

Here are some common pushback voices and sample responses. Adapt the wording to fit your own personality, beliefs, and situation."

- **Teacher**

  We do not talk about things like that in class.

  Response: *I understand. At home, we explore it as a way to notice feelings and build empathy. It is not about schoolwork—it is about family connection.*

- **Pastor or Religious Leader**

  That sounds unbiblical / unspiritual.

  Response: *For us, it is simply about listening with love. Scripture itself shows God revealing hidden things. We weigh everything by whether it leads to peace, humility, and compassion.*

- **Grandparent or Older Relative**

  We never did that when we raised kids.

Response: *You are right—and I honor what you did. Today, we're learning new ways of listening and connecting. It is still about love and family, just in a form that works for us.*

- **Medical or Mental-Health Professional**

  That sounds like imagination or even delusion.

  Response: *We treat it as a mindfulness practice, like meditation. If it ever became distressing, we'd seek support. Right now, it is playful and life-giving.*

- **Friend or Neighbor**

  That's just weird / not real.

  Response: *I get it—it can sound unusual. For us, it is simply about listening better and building trust. Even if you call it intuition, the result is the same.*

- **Co-Parent or Spouse**

  I do not want our child confused by this.

  Response: *I hear your concern. My intent is not to confuse, but to give our child tools for empathy and calm. We can go slowly and keep checking in together.*

---

3. Addressing Disagreement:

When you sense resistance, think of building a BRIDGE, not a wall:

The BRIDGE Approach

- **B—Breathe**. Pause before reacting.
- **R—Respect**. Acknowledge their viewpoint, even if you disagree.
- **I—Inquire**. Ask curious questions: "What makes you feel that way?"
- **D—Describe**. Share your own experience calmly and briefly.

- **G—Ground**. Keep your child's well-being and love at the center.

- **E—Exit gracefully**. If the conversation turns unkind, bow out without conflict. You can always revisit the topic later if the relationship feels safe.

---

4. Is Telepathy Safe and Spiritual?

For some, telepathy feels natural and affirming. For others, it raises questions: Is this spiritually safe? Is it ethical? What will people think?

The truth is that every culture, faith, and wisdom tradition has language for this gift. Some call it intuition, inner knowing, discernment, charisma, body language, or listening with the heart.

Modern science speaks of mirror neurons, the heart–brain field, and nonlocal consciousness. Whatever the name, the underlying reality is the same: human beings are wired to connect beyond words.

Across Faiths and Traditions

- **Christianity**: Scripture shows God revealing hidden things (Matt. 9:4; 2 Kgs. 6:12). The capacity itself is neutral—it is the intention that determines whether it is used in the spirit of love (Gal. 5:22–23) or not.

- **Judaism**: The Hebrew prophets often "heard" God's word internally and saw visions of what others could not.

- **Islam**: The Qur'an describes God (Allah) as Al-'Alim, 'The All-Knowing,' whose knowledge encompasses what is visible and invisible. Many believers understand this to include guidance and insight that can come in ways beyond ordinary senses.

- **Hinduism and Buddhism**: Yogic and meditative traditions recognize siddhis (spiritual abilities), including telepathic insight, as natural outgrowths of inner practice.

- **Indigenous and shamanic traditions**: Listening without words is central to community life, ceremony, and connection with the land.

What Truly Matters

The channel is not the issue, it's how we use it that matters most. A hammer can build a house or break a window; fire can warm or destroy. The same could be said about telepathy. The core questions are:

- Does it foster peace, humility and love?
- Or, does it lead to fear, pride, or manipulation?

Telepathic individuals are going to be more aware of others who may be using telepathy in a selfish, narcissistic or unsafe way. We have been given this for our benefit and to benefit others.

Ethics

- **Consent**—Healthy telepathic connection honors the willingness of both parties.
- **Intention**—Use your gift to strengthen relationships, not to control or intrude.
- **Integration**—If experiences ever feel overwhelming, seek balance through prayer, grounding, or talking with a mentor, counselor, or spiritual guide.

---

5. Principles for Safe and Respectful Practice

- **Use friendly language.** In some circles, "telepathy" raises eyebrows. Try gentler words like intuition, discernment, or heart-listening.
- **Keep love at the center.** Let your deepest values be the measure: does it foster peace, humility, and compassion?
- **Avoid risky methods.** Stay clear of practices that feel manipulative, coercive, or fear-based. Keep the channel clean.
- **Honor consent and privacy.** Never "probe" without permission. Treat the inner life as a private room, opened only by invitation.

- **Stay accountable**. Share impressions humbly, with the willingness to say "I could be wrong." Look for confirmation, not control.

- **Seek help when needed**. If experiences ever feel overwhelming or distressing, reach out to a qualified mental-health professional or trusted mentor.

A Universal Birthright

Telepathy is not a threat to faith, culture, or family values. It is a human birthright. Every child is born with it wide open; most adults simply forget. Choosing to remember is not about joining a religion or leaving one. It is about reclaiming the natural ability to listen with the whole self.

---

6. Your Child, Your Sacred Role

Parenting a telepathic child is not a task to fear—it is an invitation to remember. You are not raising your child in isolation, and you are not at the mercy of critics, institutions, or cultural doubt. You are standing in a role that stretches back through the millennia: parent as protector, parent as teacher, parent as the first and lasting home.

Your child does not need you to be flawless. They need to feel your love. Telepathically, that love is the field in which they grow—an invisible embrace that says "You are cherished, you are safe, you belong."

When you encounter skepticism, remember: others may have opinions, but only you carry the sacred responsibility of guiding your child's inner life. When you feel uncertain, remember: even small gestures of love ripple powerfully through the bond you share. And when you feel weary, remember: love covers many faults, and connection is always stronger than perfection.

As you practice the tools in this book, let your joy lead. Celebrate the little moments when your child senses what you feel, or when you share a silent understanding together. These moments are not only milestones—they are the very fabric of trust, empathy, and lifelong connection.

Go forward anchored in this truth: you are enough, your love is enough, and your child is more than enough. Together, you are part of a remembering that cannot be undone.

---

7. Guidelines for Safe Telepathy

- Always honor **consent**—never intrude without permission.

- Check your **intention**—does this build love, trust, and peace?

- Stay **grounded**—if overwhelmed, use prayer, meditation, or centering.

- Keep it **relational**—telepathy strengthens connection, not control.

- Seek **balance**—if experiences feel too strong, talk with a trusted mentor, counselor, or spiritual guide.

BONUS SECTIONS

.

Welcome to the Bonus Materials

You have just completed the heart of this book — the science, the stories, the guidance, and the remembrance. Now we shift from understanding to experiencing. The following pages are designed to help you *feel* the principles you have learned, not just read about them. These activities give your family — yes, the whole family, even between adults — a way to practice intuition, telepathy, coherence, and energetic awareness in a way that is simple, joyful, and natural.

These tools are intentionally light, playful, and flexible. Children learn best through curiosity and movement, and adults learn best when the pressure is low and connection leads the way. Nothing has to be perfect. Nothing needs to "work" on the first try. What matters is creating a space where everyone feels safe, respected, and free to explore.

Let these pages become your family's laboratory of wonder — a place where telepathy is practiced, intuition grows strong, and confidence begins to bloom. What follows will guide you gently into that experience.

Bonus Material

Consent Matters

Every practice session begins with readiness, aligned intentions, and mutual agreement. The simple "Are you ready?" and a "Yes" in response honor the energy exchange. If either partner feels tired, distracted, or unwilling, then skip the practice for now. Presence and consent create the safe container in which true listening happens.

Adaptations

There is no template or set of instructions that fits every telepathy session you practice together. So all the activities in this book are created as general guidelines. Let your sense of love and the beginner's subtle hints of telepathy steer you toward success.

Sessions can include multiple people: siblings, other adults, and even pets. This creates an opportunity and space for practice. Repeat it as often as you want.

Quiet Awareness

Before You Begin:

Purpose: Build self awareness and co regulation while tracking comfort over time; establish a safe, simple, playful field for telepathy practice.

Time: 5-10 minutes (short is fine for young children)

Materials: Setup Checklist; Results Scale; Pen/Pencil

Preparation and Overview

There is a Setup Worksheet at the end of this short practice. It has the image of a phone. Take a picture and print a copy. As you start the session together check the boxes and ask your child, "Are you ready?" When the session is over, reflect on what you sensed and how thoughts flowed in your mind. It may seem like no telepathy occurred or maybe some did, but it is difficult to be sure. Pick a score regarding the 'newness' of this session. Do not overthink and try to be "right." Record the score that came to mind when you first considered the question. Did anything seem different?

Tone to Set

Safety, simplicity, and play.

Consent

1. Read aloud: "Are you ready to begin?" Proceed only when both say "Yes."
2. If either feels "not yet," take a slow breath together, stretch, or wait until readiness returns.

Practice (Quiet Connection)

1. Sit together in shared silence (start with ~1 minute; increase as needed).
2. Notice: ambient sounds; emotions and body sensations; subtle senses; passing thoughts, temperature, etc.
3. End with a gentle smile or nod.

Reflection

1. Ask: "Did this feel new in any way?"
2. Child marks Yes/No on the Setup Worksheet.
3. (Optional) Each tells about something new they noticed.

Gentle Scoring & Celebrate

1. Take ~30 seconds to compare notes; look for overlaps, not mistakes.
2. Even one overlap is evidence of a connection.
3. Celebrate with a smile, high five, or shared laugh. (Joy amplifies signal strength.)

Age Adaptations

1. Younger children: keep quiet to 20–30 seconds; repeat the session if desired.
2. Older children: extend gradually to 2–3 minutes; add one extra reflection prompt.

Recordkeeping (1 line each)

1. Date/Time.
2. Newness Score: From 0 to 5 (from not new to quite different).
3. Your scores may not be equal, but partial overlaps are a success!

Experiencing Newness

Keep a log of the sessions and ratings. Newness ratings can be influenced by many things. "Newness" is the presence of a sense or knowing unlike prior sessions.

You might sense subtle variations of newness such as novelty, originality, or freshness. It may seem wispy and uncertain. This gets scored as a 1. Even this score is a success, and if it is 'wrong,' it is a success because you are engaging and investing in your future together.

Celebrate the Attempt

Emphasize that the worksheet is not a test. It is a record of exploration. Every try strengthens awareness, regardless of the number circled.

Keep your records for review and reflection over time. Looking back at these worksheets shows progress and patterns. Some families keep them in a binder or folder to review together.

Setup Worksheet

Prepare the Space:

☐ Phones off

☐ Comfortable seating

☐ Uncluttered

Are you ready to begin?

Did this practice feel new?

○ YES   ○ NO

Date: _____

Name: _____

Circle your rating after the practice session is over. How new did this seem to be?

Newness: | 0 | 1 | 2 | 3 | 4 | 5 |

0: not new, 5: quite different.
Your scores may not be equal, but partial overlaps are success!

Quiet Handshake

PRACTICE 1:

Purpose: Tune into subtle, nonverbal signals through touch; develop micro signal awareness via pulse coupling and tactile entrainment.

Time: 3–6 minutes (short rounds work well)

Materials: Print a Scoring Sheet. A timer is optional

The Shared Pulse

This exercise is designed to help you and your partner tune into subtle, nonverbal signals through touch. It is a different approach from exercises that rely on visual or verbal cues. It uses the principles of pulse coupling and tactile entrainment to help you connect on a deeper, more rhythmic level.

HOW TO DO IT

Setup:

Sit together, side by side, in a quiet space. Gently rest your wrists or hands so they are lightly touching.

Consent:

1. Ask and answer: "Are you ready?"—both partners say "Yes" before starting.

Consent:

1. Ask and answer: "Are you ready?"—both partners say "Yes" before starting.

2. One partner silently chooses a subtle pulsed rhythm.

3. The partner who chose the rhythm should now physically send it through the shared touch, maintaining a steady pace for 30-60 seconds.

4. The other partner should simply relax and allow their body to synchronize with the rhythm without actively "trying" to match it.

5. Switch roles and repeat the exercise. Afterward, you can discuss what you noticed during the practice.

Advanced versions:

1. You can do this exercise using telepathy. Start with your wrists or hands so they are lightly touching and transmit the rhythm telepathically.

2. Over time, you may be able to do this when far apart. This can become the foundation for long-distance healing to deliver well-established modalities like Reiki and Bowen Therapy.

Why It Is New:

This practice uses pulse coupling and tactile entrainment, which are different from the visual or verbal focus of the Toolbox exercises. It trains both partners to "tune into" micro-signals and shared rhythms.

Gentle Scoring & Celebrate

1. Compare notes for ~30 seconds; look for overlaps, not errors.

2. Even one shared detail indicates connection.

3. Celebrate with a smile, high five, or shared laugh.

Closing Note:

The aim of this exercise is to expand body awareness and build adult-child coherence without tools. Notice the subtle shift: When two nervous systems fall into rhythm together, a field of telepathic listening opens more easily.

The Quiet Handshake
Scoring Sheet

Timing Box

○ 30 Seconds

○ 45 Seconds

○ 60 Seconds

Role Tracker

Sender: _____

Receiver: _____

Sensations / Accuracy Notes

_____

_____

_____

_____

Results Scale

Circle your rating after the practice:

0	1	2	3	4	5

> *0= no match, 5 = perfectly synchronized rhythm.*
> *Even partial overlap = success!*

Symbol Seeds Lexicon

PRACTICE 2:

Aim: Create a shared symbolic language that improves signal clarity over time.

Description:

Telepathy often comes through in images, feelings, or impressions—not words. By building a personal "symbol deck," you and your partner create a unique telepathic vocabulary that grows stronger with use.

Steps:

1. Each partner chooses 12 simple symbols. These can be objects, animals, shapes, or memories (for example: tree, sun, spiral, bird, key, wave).

2. Draw or write these on small cards, or keep them listed on a sheet of paper.

3. The sender silently chooses one symbol and holds it in mind with strong feeling for 30 seconds.

4. The receiver looks at the 12-symbol list and chooses the one that feels most "alive" or "pulled."

5. Compare results and note matches.

6. Switch roles.

Why It Is New:

Unlike classic Zener card experiments, this practice uses personalized symbols that carry emotional resonance. This emotional charge strengthens signal clarity, making the exercise more effective and fun.

Closing Note:

Over time, you may notice certain symbols becoming "hot spots" that almost always transmit clearly. This is how a private telepathic lexicon develops—your shared symbolic language.

Symbol Seeds Worksheet

Preparation:

Take pictures of the symbol cards with your phone. Print them and cut them out. Print the Results Log too. Review and discuss the shapes so you have names for them.

How to Use the Symbol Seeds Chart:

1. Choose a Sender and a Receiver.
2. The Sender secretly picks one of the 12 symbol cards.
3. The Receiver stays quiet and relaxed.

Send the Symbol.

1. The Sender looks at the symbol and imagines it clearly for 30 seconds.

2. Picture it big, bright, and full of energy.

Receive 1. The Receiver chooses the symbol they feel or imagine the most strongly.

Record the Round.

Write the symbol the Sender chose in the "Symbol Sent" column.

Create your own symbol cards

1. There is a set of empty boxes after the ones with shapes. You can use these to make your own symbol cards. Print several copies. Draw symbols in the boxes, then cut them out like the others.

Advanced versions:

1. To explore and test your skills, draw or paste a picture in a box, or use numbers and letters. Test your skills with colors, too. You may be better with some than others. Have fun and celebrate the time together.

Symbol Seeds Results Log

Sender: _____

Receiver: _____

Session Date: _____ Accuracy: _____ %

Write reflections on the back

Round	Symbol Sent	Symbol Received	Match	Note
1				
2				
3				
4				
5				

Object Echoes

PRACTICE 3:

Aim: Strengthen nonverbal sensory imaging and reception.

Description:

Every object carries a field of impressions: texture, weight, temperature, and even an "aura" of use. This practice trains both partners to send and receive those impressions without words.

Steps:

1. Gather two opaque envelopes and place a different household object in each (for example: a coin, a feather, a button, a small stone, a small toy).

2. The sender chooses one envelope, holds its object for 30 seconds, and silently focuses on its qualities: heavy/light, smooth/rough, warm/cool, hard/soft. Do not send its name.

3. The sender transmits those sensory "echoes" mentally and the receiver tunes in.

4. When the time is over, place the envelopes side by side.

5. The receiver then chooses which envelope contains the object that was being described.

6. Switch roles and repeat the activity.

Why It Is New:

Instead of asking for names or mental pictures, this practice emphasizes pure sensation—how an object feels rather than what it is. This builds sensitivity to subtle sensory transfer.

Closing Note:

Accuracy grows when you relax and allow impressions to drift in. Do not force an answer; simply allow impressions to arise. Notice which senses arrive first—some people perceive texture, others weight, others temperature. Trust your unique channel.

Object Echoes Results Log

Check all that you notice

☐ Weight (heavy / light)
☐ Temperature (warm / cool)
☐ Texture (smooth / rough)
☐ Texture (hard / soft)
☐ Size (big / small)

Sender: _____

Receiver: _____

Session Date: _____ Accuracy: _____%

Write reflections on the back

Round	Symbol Sent	Symbol Received	Match	Note
1				
2				
3				
4				
5				

Timeline Pings

PRACTICE 4:

Aim: Practice sending and receiving moments anchored in time.

Description:

Memory carries an energetic stamp. By choosing a specific moment from the past day, you learn to transmit not just images or feelings but the time-coded essence of an experience. This strengthens accuracy and makes telepathy more tangible.

Steps:

1. The sender silently selects a moment from the last 24 hours. Anchor it with a clock time (for example, yesterday at 4:15 p.m.).

2. Focus on three strong qualities of that moment—sights, sounds, or feelings. Hold them vividly in mind.

3. Send the "ping" of that memory toward your partner for 30-60 seconds.

4. The receiver writes down three impressions that arise (words, images, feelings).

5. Compare. Even partial matches—a sound, a mood, or a color—are signs of connection.

6. Switch roles.

Why It Is New:

Unlike other exercises, Timeline Pings anchor telepathic impressions to a specific time stamp, which trains both precision and discernment.

Closing Note:

When successful, this practice feels like stepping into someone else's memory for a brief instant. Even if the details do not fully align, the feeling tone of the moment often transmits clearly.

Timeline Pings Worksheet

Time Target

Chosen Time: _____
(for example, 4:15 PM yesterday)

Three-Word Prompt Sheet (Receiver)

1. _____

2. _____

3. _____

Match Counter

☐ Partial overlap (1 detail matched)

☐ Strong overlap (2 details matched)

☐ Complete overlap (all 3 details matched)

Reflection Space

A. How did the impressions feel? Were they more emotional, visual, or sensory?

B. Keep it minimal so kids and adults do not confuse it with the main activity.

Field Writing

PRACTICE 5:

Aim: Link subtle intention with hand movement.

Description:

Sometimes telepathic exchange bypasses words and images, showing up instead as movement. This practice uses free-flow writing to capture the energetic "field" shared between two people.

Steps:

1. Both partners sit with pen and paper.

2. The sender chooses a simple mental shape (circle, triangle, wave, zigzag) and holds it clearly in mind for 30-45 seconds.

3. At the same time, both partners keep their pens moving continuously across the page—no stopping, no lifting, letting the hand wander freely.

4. After time is up, compare the lines, curves, or angles on the two pages.

5. Switch roles and repeat with a new shape.

Why It Is New:

Instead of drawing a picture, Field Writing focuses on motion entrainment. The energy of the sender's shape influences the receiver's hand patterns, creating overlaps in angles, curves, or flow.

Closing Note:

Do not expect identical drawings. Look for resemblances in slope, rhythm, or direction. Even subtle similarities are evidence that you shared a field.

Field Writing Worksheet

Use the area below to draw your free-flow writing, or for more space use a blank sheet of paper.

Similarity Slider (0-5)

> *Circle the number that best shows how closely your lines matched your partner's. 0= no match, 5 = perfectly synchronized rhythm. Even partial overlap = success!*

0	1	2	3	4	5

Reflection Prompts

A. How did it feel to let your hand move freely?

_____

B. Did you notice any emotions or body sensations?

_____

C. Were the lines smooth, jagged, or repetitive?

_____

Taste Tag

PRACTICE 6:

Aim: Train cross-sensory imagery and reception.

Description:

Most telepathic practices lean on sight and sound, but taste is just as powerful a channel. By using imagined flavors, you invite the brain and body to communicate through a less-expected pathway, which often sharpens signal clarity.

Steps:

1. Prepare a simple "taste deck"—six cards labeled: sweet, sour, salty, bitter, spicy, and umami.

2. The sender secretly selects one card and spends 30 seconds vividly imagining that taste—lemon for sour, honey for sweet, chili pepper for spicy, etc.

3. Hold the taste in mind as if you were really experiencing it. Notice saliva, texture, intensity.

4. The receiver relaxes and senses which taste feels most present.

5. The receiver chooses one of the six cards.

6. Compare, then switch roles.

Why It Is New:

Taste Tag bypasses visual images and taps into the gustatory sense—an unusual but effective channel for telepathic practice. Because taste is tied to strong memory and body response, it often produces clearer results.

Closing Note:

Do not worry if you do not "taste" anything directly. Many people receive flavors as colors, textures, or even emotions. For example, "sweet" may feel warm and soft, while "bitter" may feel sharp or heavy. Trust whatever arrives.

Taste Tag Worksheet

Role Log

Sender:

_____

Receiver:

_____

Session Date: _____

Round	Symbol Sent	Symbol Received	Match	Note
1				
2				
3				
4				
5				

Reflection Space

Note any sense of taste, color, mood, odor, or sensations that arose.

Circle the number that best shows how closely your "tastes" matched your partner's. 0= no match, 5 = perfectly synchronized rhythm. Even partial overlap = success!

0	1	2	3	4	5

Flavor Facts

Sweet
Sweet tastes like sugar or honey. It makes foods like candy, fruit, and desserts yummy and fun to eat.

Sour
Sour tastes sharp and tangy, like lemons or limes. It makes your mouth pucker up!

Salty
Salty tastes like salt. You find it in foods like popcorn, pretzels, and potato chips.

Spicy
Spicy feels hot or tingly on your tongue. Chili peppers and hot sauce make foods spicy.

Bitter
Bitter tastes strong and can seem a little yucky at first. Foods like unsweetened, dark chocolate, black coffee, and some leafy greens are bitter.

Umami
Umami is the "savory taste." It makes food taste rich and cozy, like soup, cheese, mushrooms, or cooked meat.

Sour

Sweet

Salty

Spicy

Bitter

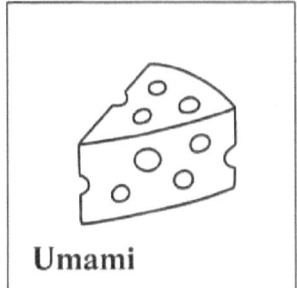

Umami

Sour

Sweet

Salty

Spicy

Bitter

Umami

Color Drift

PRACTICE 7:

Aim: Improve fine-grained reception using subtle color variations.

Description:

Colors carry vibration, and our nervous systems respond to them instinctively. This practice uses a smooth gradient of color to train precision in receiving impressions beyond basic "red, green, and blue."

Prepare

This activity uses color strips with gradients from light to dark. There are paint chip supply sets for children online. You may also find them in paint stores. If you would like, you can create them using paint, pencils, chalk, or crayons. This would be a great way to discuss art and painting.

For a younger child using a color gradient strip with 6 colors, number the colors 1 through 6 from light to dark. For advanced practice and a more detailed gradient range, use 0 for white, 50 for medium blue, and so on.

Print the Color Drift Worksheet or make your own. You will need several copies to record your scores as sender and receiver. Be creative. This is just a simple way to get you started.

Steps:

1. Place the color strip between the sender and receiver. Discuss the worksheet and the actions in the activity. Keep it simple.

2. The sender slowly drifts their attention along the strip for 30 seconds, then stops silently at one place and notes the number for that choice.

3. The sender holds the chosen color firmly in mind, noticing its depth, brightness, and emotional tone for 30 seconds, or as long as you would like.

4. The receiver scans the color strip and "listens" for the color that feels most alive or "calling."

5. Compare choices. Even being close shows clear sensitivity.

6. Switch roles and repeat with another gradient (different color family).

How to Use the Bar Graph

1. You can use this in various ways. For the activity described above, the worksheet has a column for six practice events. Record the first round in column 1: Put an 'S' by the number the Sender focused on and 'R' for the number the Receiver sensed.

2. Repeat the activity using different colors and different roles. Record the 'S' and 'R' like before. You can also record which color set was used for each session.

3. See how close you got on that turn.

4. Keep going.

5. Do the same for turns 2, 3, 4, 5, and 6.

6. Check your work. When you are done, your graph will show how you did each time!

Why It Is New:

Unlike practices that rely on shapes or objects, Color Drift focuses on fine gradations and sharpens subtle perception and accuracy. This exercise strengthens discernment by rewarding "near matches."

Closing Note:

Over time, you may notice you consistently "land" near the sender's choice. This shows your telepathic sense is tuning in to subtler frequencies. Celebrate the time together, as well as any hint or degree of telepathy.

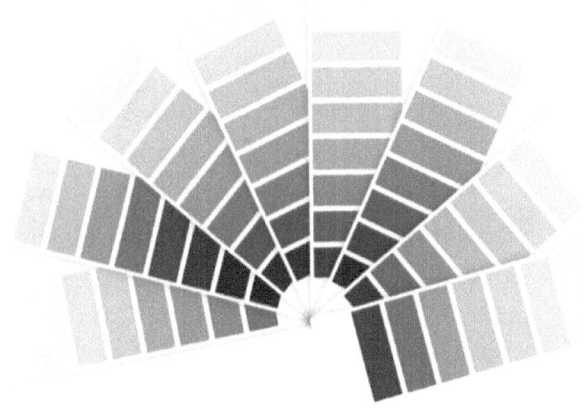

Color Drift Worksheet

Role Log

Date: _____ .

Sender: _____ .

Receiver: _____ .

Reflection Space

Note any impressions that arose — taste, color, mood, scent, temperature, or any other sensory or emotional signal.

_____

_____

_____

Sense of Newness:

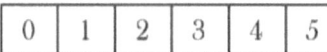

Debrief, Progress Tracker, and Next Steps

Why Debrief Matters

Telepathy improves when both partners reflect together.
Debriefing ensures the process feels safe, playful, and encouraging
rather than pressured.

Three-Step Debrief

- Notice—Say out loud one thing you observed, even if small
(a color flash, a mood shift, a body sensation).

- Name—Give it a simple label so your partner knows how you
experienced it.

- Normalize—Treat every detail as valid, even if it seems odd
or mismatched. Over time, patterns emerge from what once felt
random.

Troubleshooting Common Blocks

- Fatigue—Rest first, keep sessions short.

- Over-effort—If you strain to "get it right," accuracy drops.
Relax.

- Distraction—Clear the space; outside noise interferes with
subtle sensing.

• Self-doubt—Confidence grows with practice; remember, even near misses count.

Adult Self-Repair Practices

• Unhook—Shake out your hands, move your body to reset.

• Reset—Take three deep breaths; imagine clearing static.

• Open—Place one hand over the heart and silently affirm: "I am open to receive and share."

Progress Tracking

For best results, work with 2 practices per week for 3 weeks. Record accuracy, reflections, and impressions in your workbook or on the printable template page. Celebrate improvements—small steps add up.

Completion Certificate

At the end of your practice cycle, create your own playful "Telepathy Certificate." Honor the effort, not just the results. Recognition builds confidence and joy.

Practice Tracker Table

Week	Practice	Accuracy (%)	Reflections/Notes
Week 1	Practice 1		
Week 1	Practice 2		
Week 2	Practice 1		
Week 2	Practice 2		
Week 3	Practice 1		
Week 3	Practice 2		

Reflection Prompts for Each Session

Week 1, 2 and 3

Practice 1 and 2

- What did I notice?

- What felt surprising?

- What can I try next time?

Introduction to the Certificates

These certificates are designed to celebrate growth, effort, and the joyful journey your family is taking together. Telepathy, intuition, coherence, and energetic awareness all strengthen through practice, curiosity, and connection. Every time your child (or your whole family) engages with the activities in this book, they are building confidence, trust, and heart-centered communication.

Use these certificates whenever it feels right.
You may fill one out after a single practice session, after a week of consistent play, or at the end of your family's telepathy adventure. Some families will use them to honor special breakthroughs, while others will enjoy creating a certificate for every activity they complete.

There is no right or wrong way to use them.

The purpose is simple: to recognize progress, celebrate effort, and encourage your child's natural intuitive abilities.

Whether your child is guessing symbols, sensing feelings, practicing coherence, or tuning in with a sibling or parent, these certificates are a reminder that their inner gifts matter. Frame them, place them on the refrigerator, or tuck them into a keepsake folder—whatever helps reinforce joy and pride.

Most of all, let these certificates be a reflection of the love, connection, and trust you are building together.

Every step, no matter how small, is worth celebrating.

Certificate Of
Congratulations

This Certificate is awarded to:

Name: _____

For: _____

Date: _____ Signed by: _____

Certificate Of
Congratulations

This Certificate is awarded to:

Name: _____

For: _____

Date: _____ Signed by: _____

Certificate Of Congratulations

This Certificate is awarded to:

Name: _____

For: _____

Date: _____

Signed by: _____

Certificate Of
Congratulations

This Certificate is awarded to:

Name: _____

For: _____

Date: _____

_____
Signed By

Certificate Of Congratulations

This Certificate is awarded to:

Name: _____

For: _____

Date: _____

Signed by,

_____

ABOUT THE AUTHOR
Susan V. Whittaker, PhD, DMs, MS

Dr. Susan Whittaker is a pioneer in the fields of intuition development, energy medicine, and conscious parenting. With over 25 years of experience teaching first grade, she brings a grounded, compassionate understanding of children's emotional and developmental needs. Her classroom became a living lab for recognizing and supporting intuitive and telepathic children long before the mainstream caught on.

In addition to her decades in education, Dr. Whittaker is a master dowser, medical intuitive, and crystal therapist. She is the creator of the Broad Spectrum DeTOX program and the author of several groundbreaking works in vibrational health and metaphysical science. Raised in the remote Alaskan wilderness and trained from birth in shamanic healing, Susan blends ancient wisdom with modern science. She guides families into higher states of connection and coherence.

Through her books, workshops, and global speaking engagements, Dr. Whittaker empowers caregivers to honor their child's inner knowing and support multidimensional communication. Together, they can co-create a future grounded in love, light, and listening.

Contact: Sue@DeTOXalot.com
Website: www.DeTOXalot.com

Susan V. Whittaker's Dowsers Guides

General Dowsing

Allergies: Volume 1, Volume 2

Pets

The Care and Feeding of Chakras

Sentient Entities

Angels

Invisible Entities

Aliens

Visible Entities

Star Trek

Holistic Health

Issues and Needs

Products and Providers

Remedies

The Complete Guide to Crystal Therapy:
  Volume 1, Volume 2

Diving Deep into the Ocean of the Mind: a Guide for Exploring, Empowering and Elevating Your Energy Using Your Subconscious Mind

Dowsing Docs

General Practice
  Remedies
  Products and Providers

Dentists

Homeopaths

Veterinarians: Volume 1, Volume 2